# RURAL SOCIOLOGY

## A Bibliography of Bibliographies

by
Judy Berndt

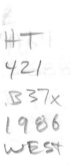

The Scarecrow Press, Inc.
Metuchen, N.J., & London
1986

Library of Congress Cataloging-in-Publication Data

Berndt, Judy, 1942-
    Rural sociology.

    Includes indexes.
    1. Bibliography--Bibliography--Sociology, Rural.
I. Title.
Z7164.S688B47  1986    [HT421]   016.0163077'2    85-26070
ISBN 0-8108-1860-4

Manufactured in the United States of America

# ACKNOWLEDGMENTS

I would like to thank the administration of the Colorado State University Libraries for granting me leave at times throughout the past year to work on this bibliography.

I am grateful to Julie Wessling and her staff in the CSU Libraries' Inter-Library Loan Department for their competence, cheerfulness, and humor.

I would like to express my thanks to Bob Berndt, Marge Hill, Terry Hubbard, John Redmond, and Emily Taylor for their on-going support in my life.

# CONTENTS

# INTRODUCTION

This bibliography attempts to list and annotate all English
language bibliographies in rural sociology published separately since 1970. Arrangement is by author within fifteen
subject divisions. There is a concluding personal and corporate name index, a title index, and a geographical index.
Readers should be aware that not all items fall neatly into
only one category. Thus bibliographies on women in rural
development, for example, could be placed in either the section on "women" or the section on "development." There
are other items that could also be placed with equal logic in
more than one category. They have not been cross-referenced.

In the course of compiling the bibliography many
items were examined and rejected. I attempted to include
only those items that are concerned exclusively with social
aspects of rural life. Thus bibliographies on biological or
technical aspects of rural or agricultural development were
not included, nor were bibliographies on agricultural economics. Likewise, I did not normally include bibliographies
that only partially concern rural life and development--works
on economic development that only partially relate to rural
areas were not listed, for example, nor were bibliographies
on the involvement of women in both urban and rural development. In a few cases I made exceptions to these selection
principles.

In identifying titles for consideration, I searched
numerous indexes both manually and by computer. The
most fruitful of these indexes were those produced by the
Commonwealth Agricultural Bureaux and the (U.S.) National
Agricultural Library. I also searched the RLIN data base
of the Research Libraries Group. Finally, I spent eight

days using the Land Tenure Center Library at the University of Wisconsin-Madison. This enabled me to include some fugitive items that would have been otherwise unavailable.

The annotations I have written describe the scope, time period covered, size, and arrangement of each of the bibliographies. If a bibliography is itself annotated, either its title or my annotation will so indicate. All quotations in the annotations are taken from the author's introductory remarks. The exception to this is ERIC items in which quotations are usually from the Clearinghouse abstract.

In order to make the bibliography as up-to-date as possible, some items are included without annotations. In a few instances these were not available through Inter-Library Loan; usually they have been only recently identified.

Items with an "ED" number are available from the Educational Resources Information Center. Ordering information is available in Resources in Education and from ERIC Document Reproduction Service, P.O. Box 190, Arlington, VA, 22210.

1. International Labour Organization. Bibliography of the
   Situation of Old People in Rural Areas (1956-1970).
   D.23.1970. 18p.
   Unavailable for annotation.

2. Kim, Paul K.H., and H. Lamprey. A Bibliography on
   Rural Aging. Gerontology Publication Series, no.
   1979-1. Lexington: Mental Health and Rural Gerontology Project, College of Social Professions, University of Kentucky, 1979.
   Books, journal articles, government documents and
   technical reports as well as unpublished research papers are
   included in this bibliography. The bibliography is not restricted by date of publication although the majority of items
   were published in the 1970's. Most citations are to works
   dealing with the U.S. rural aged. The subject emphasis is
   mental health but related topics such as transportation, nutrition, etc. are included.
   The 553 items in the bibliography are arranged in no
   apparent order. Each entry is assigned one or more subject
   codes for ten topics, such as housing, mental health, human
   services, etc. There is a concluding author index.

3. Krout, John A. The Rural Elderly: An Annotated Bibliography of Social Science Research. Westport, CT:
   Greenwood Press, 1983. xi + 123p.
   "... This annotated bibliography has been compiled to
   provide a comprehensive listing (through 1982) and description of both pure and applied research in the area of the
   rural elderly." Only works on the elderly population within
   the United States are included.
   Listed in the bibliography are citations to "journal
   articles, books, book chapters, government reports and
   hearings, theses, dissertations, grant reports, conference

proceedings, conference paper presentations, bibliographies,
experiment station publications, and unpublished manuscripts."
Under 29 subject headings, citations are arranged alphabetically by author. There are author and geographical
indexes.

4.  Wilkinson, Carroll Wetzel; Graham D. Rowles; and Betty
    Maxwell. Aging in Rural America:  A Comprehensive
    Annotated Bibliography 1975-1981. [Morgantown]:
    West Virginia University Gerontology Center, 1982.
    ix + 119p.
    "This bibliography documents and evaluates as com-
prehensively as possible what has been printed in the United
States about the rural elderly since 1975." The 350 works
listed include published books, journal articles, conference
proceedings, etc. as well as unpublished dissertations and
other research papers.
    "Users will notice that there are two basic sections in
the bibliography:  an author section with critical annotations,
and a subject section which takes the publications discovered
and analyzed in the first section and divides them into twenty-
two topic areas."

5.  Yenerall, Joseph D., and Sondra F. Haynes. The Rural
    Aged in America:  An Annotated Bibliography with
    Supplementary References. Albany, NY:  Institute
    for Public Policy Alternatives, 1975. iii + 52 leaves.
    Primarily listing monographs, periodical articles, and
government documents from the 1960's and 1970's, this bibliography on the rural aged in the United States is arranged
into eight subject chapters:  "Perspectives on the Rural
Aged," "Work, Leisure and Retirement," "Family/Kinship Relationships of Rural Aged," "Economic Status of Rural Aged,"
"Housing, Transportation and the Rural Aged," "Health Status and Care of the Rural Aged," "Programs/Services and
the Rural Aged," and "Some Supplementary References."
There are no indexes.

CRIME

6. Hubbard, Robert D., et al. Rural Crime and Criminal
   Justice: A Selected Bibliography. Washington, D.C.:
   National Institute of Justice, U.S. Dept. of Justice,
   1980. ix + 57p. ED 209 008.
   Items listed in this bibliography are part of the National Criminal Justice Reference Service Collection and include government documents and technical reports, journal
articles, and dissertations and other unpublished papers and
reports.
   Not limited by date, the citations also include lengthy
annotations. The bibliography is organized into five subject
chapters: "Rural Crime: Nature and Extent," "Rural Criminal Justice," "Rural Crime Prevention and Law Enforcement,"
"Rural Adjudication and Corrections," and "Rural Juvenile
Justice and Delinquency Prevention." Within chapters arrangement is alphabetical by author. There are indexes by
author, title, and subject.

7. Van Buren, David P. Crime, Delinquency, and Criminal
   Justice Within the Rural Context: A Bibliography.
   Public Administration Series, no. P-1626. Monticello,
   IL: Vance Bibliographies, 1985. 62p.
   This bibliography is intended to provide "students
and researchers with a comprehensive list of scholarly works
relating to crime, delinquency, and the administration of
justice within the context of rural community.... It is arranged, by topic, into thirteen categories, and for all but
three of these categories every effort was made to provide a
comprehensive and exhaustive listing of existing works. The
three categories for which the list of citations was only selective are: (1) Drug and Alcohol Abuse in Rural Areas;
(2) Mental Illness in Rural Areas; and (3) Legal Aid, Indi-
gent Defense, and Legal Services for the Rural Poor." The
bibliography does not limit itself to the United States.

8. Warner, John R. Rural Crime: A Bibliography. Public
    Administration Series, no. P-77. Monticello, IL:
    Vance Bibliographies, 1978. 13p.
       The emphasis in this bibliography is on rural crime
 in twentieth-century America. Books, articles, state and
 federal government reports, dissertations, and National
 Criminal Justice Reference Service documents are arranged
 in one alphabetical list by author. All aspects of rural
 crime are included, although the administration of criminal
 justice is dealt with only slightly.

9. Abdullah, Mohammad Mohiuddin. Shawnirvar Programme
   in Bangladesh: A Selected Bibliography. Dacca:
   Learned Society, 1980. 30p.
   The subject of this partially annotated bibliography
is rural development; the emphasis is on Pakistan university
and government reports published in the 1970's. The last
four pages list journal articles. Arrangement is alphabetical
by author. There are no indexes.

10. Administration of Agricultural Development: A Selected
   List of References for A.I.D. Technicians. Prepared
   by Office of Development Administration, Bureau for
   Technical Assistance, in Cooperation with A.I.D.
   Reference Center. Washington, D.C.: [U.S.]
   Agency for International Development, 1971. vi +
   13p.
   "This bibliography, one of a series designed to provide a guide to the publications of AID and other agencies
working in the field of development assistance, focuses on
the broad administrative-management aspects of agriculture
in the emerging nations. Selection of materials has been
limited mainly to the most important publications and documents that may be found in the AID Reference Center (ARC)
and the Department of State Library."
   Arrangement is by author within five subject divisions: "Agricultural Development Strategies: Administrative-
Management Element," "Agricultural Planning Systems," "Rural
Institution Building," "Delivery of Agricultural Services,"
and "Administration of Agricultural Development in Specific
Countries." There is an author, publisher, and organization
index.

11. African Bibliographic Center. Rural Development in
   Africa. Compiled by Anita Rhett et al. Current

Reading List Series, vol. 9, no. 2. Washington,
D.C.: The Center, 1972. vii + 129p.
The first in a series of six guides to development
literature on Africa, this partially annotated bibliography of
books, articles, papers, and UN documents emphasizes economic aspects of agricultural development. There are, however, entries that deal with the broader areas of rural sociology and rural development. Most items selected for the
bibliography were published between 1969 and 1972; selected
works of major importance published prior to 1969 are also
included. Works of special importance are noted with an
asterisk. Some items of interest to rural sociologists are
included in other titles in the series. For example, the
subject of rural development planning is more extensively
covered in Implementation and Administration of Development
Activities in Africa, Current Reading List Series, vol. 10,
no. 8, 1973.
The first part of the bibliography is organized into
subject chapters, the second part by geographical region
and country. Within these divisions arrangement is by
author. There are author and subject indexes.

12.    African Training and Research Centre in Administration
       for Development. Documentation Centre. Bibliogra-
       phy on Rural Development in Africa (Preliminary and
       Provisional List of Books and Periodicals Held in the
       Library of CAFRAD). Tangier, Morocco: Documen-
       tation Centre, C.A.F.R.A.D., 1970. 33 leaves.
       French and English language books and periodical
articles are listed under a variety of specific subject headings such as "rural development," "rural social structure,"
"cooperative and collective farms," etc. Most items were
published in the 1960's. Arrangement is by author within
each section. There are no indexes.

13.    Agricultural Projects Services Centre. Integrated Rural
       Development, A Bibliography. Occasional Bibliogra-
       phy, no. 2. Kathmandu, Nepal: The Centre, 1978.
       Unavailable for annotation.

14.    Agricultural Projects Services Centre. Project Manage-
       ment; A Bibliography. Occasional Bibliography, no. 5.
       Kathmandu, Nepal: The Centre, 1979. 23p.
       Unavailable for annotation.

15. Agrisnepal: Nepal Agricultural Bibliography, 1980.
     Kathmandu, Nepal: Agricultural Projects Services
     Centre, National Agricultural Documentation Centre,
     1981. xxviii + 157p.
     Unavailable for annotation.

16. Akhter, Nilufar, and Shafiq-ur-Ramhan Khan. Rural
     Development of Bangladesh: A Select Bibliography.
     BIDS Library Series, no. 20. Dacca, Bangladesh:
     Bangladesh Institute of Development Studies, 1981.
     33p.
     The 418 items in this bibliography include mono-
     graphs, conference proceedings, journal articles, theses,
     and research papers of various institutes and agencies. Not
     limited by date, the bibliography emphasizes works published
     in the 1970's. There are no indexes.

17. An Annotated Bibliography on Rural Development. Los
     Baños, Laguna, Philippines: Integrated Rural and
     Agricultural Development Program, Institute of Hu-
     man Ecology, University of the Philippines at Los
     Baños, 1975. 79p.
     This is a selected bibliography emphasizing integrated
     rural and agricultural development but including reports of
     other, prominent rural development projects. Many of the
     works included are unpublished research or evaluation re-
     ports. The bibliography is organized into seven categories:

     "1.   Pilot projects of the University of the Philippines
           at Los Baños--9 cases
      2.   Provincial, Regional, and National Development
           Pilot Programs and Projects (Philippines)--15
           cases
      3.   Overseas Development Pilot Programs--21 cases
      4.   Overseas National Development Programs--5 cases
      5.   Local Training Programs (Philippines)--6 cases
      6.   Overseas Training Programs--10 cases
      7.   Surveys--4 studies

     In addition, 30 abstracts of articles from journals
     were included to keep those concerned abreast with
     development ideas and other projects."

18. Barker, G.H. Bibliography of Literature Relating to
     Research and Development in the Agricultural Sector

of Jamaica, 1959-1979. San José, Costa Rica:
Instituto Interamericano de Cooperación para la
Agricultura, 1980. 201p.
Unavailable for annotation.

19. Barnett, Andrew; Martin Bell; and Kurt Hoffmann.
    Rural Energy and the Third World: A Review of
    Social Science Research and Technology Policy
    Problems. Oxford, U.K.: Pergamon Press, 1982,
    x + 214p.
    The 201 items selected and annotated for the bibli-
ography section of this work come from the "socio-economic
literature in English concerned with rural energy in the
Third World." Items selected were published between 1969
and 1981. Each annotation "critically evaluates the research
approaches and results of each item of literature and records
both its geographic focus and the extent of its empirical content." The bibliography includes books and journal articles
as well as unpublished papers. All material listed in the
bibliography is available from the Library of the International
Development Research Centre in Ottawa and copies of the
less accessible items can be obtained from the Library.
    The bibliography is preceded by two chapters in
which the authors discuss research issues in rural energy
development that they believe have not received sufficient
attention. The bibliography concludes with a list of significant but unannotated entries and with a subject index.

20. Bauer, A.J.J. Rural Development in the Third World,
    1970-1977. Bibliography no. 17. Wageningen, The
    Netherlands: International Institute for Land Recla-
    mation and Improvement, 1980. 191p.
    This selected, partially annotated bibliography empha-
sizes works on "participation," "small peasants," "rural wom-
en," "strategies," and "project organization." Part I of the
bibliography deals with rural development in general and is
organized into sections on bibliographies, monographs (which
includes journal articles) and conferences and reports. Part
II has a wide range of published and unpublished materials
organized by continent and country. There is an author index.

21. Benneh, George. Environment and Agricultural Develop-
    ment in the Savannah Regions of Ghana: Annotated
    Bibliography. [Legon, Ghana], 1974. xvii + 188
    leaves.

Benneh has compiled a multidisciplinary bibliography
that includes both social/economic and agricultural aspects of
development in the Savannah region of Ghana.  The bibliography includes only items available within Ghana at the time
of publication of the bibliography and thus theses and dissertations found in libraries outside the country are not included.  Books, periodical articles, UN and Ghanaian government documents, and conference proceedings are included
without regard to date of publication.

The bibliography is divided into five major sections:
"General," "Factors of Agricultural Development," "Land
Use," "Problems of Agricultural Development," and "Strategies for Agricultural Development"--as well as a variety of
sub-sections within the last four sections.  Within section or
sub-sections entries are arranged by author, are extensively
annotated, and indicate in which Ghanaian library they can
be found.  Items are listed under the most appropriate head-
ing only and are not cross-referenced.  There is an author
index at the beginning of the work.

22.  Bhatti, K.M.  Bibliography on Rural Development in
     Pakistan.  Peshawar:  Pakistan Academy for Rural
     Development, 1973.  iii + 127p.

Developed in conjunction with a 1973 International
Seminar on Rural Development, this bibliography is organized
into six subject chapters:  "Rural Pakistan:  Basic Facts &
Social Setting," "Rural Development:  Concepts," "Rural Development:  Institutions, Programmes and Policies," "Research
& Evaluation for Rural Development," "Training and Education
for Rural Development," and "Miscellaneous."

Books, periodical articles, government publications,
UN documents, dissertations, theses, and unpublished papers
are included.  Each chapter is divided into a section on books
and one on papers and articles.  Within each of these sections
entries are arranged alphabetically by author.  Selection was
not limited by date of publication although most works selected
were published after 1960.

23.  Bhatty, K.M.  Annotated Bibliography on Rural Develop-
     ment in Pakistan.  Peshawar:  Pakistan Academy for
     Rural Development, 1979.  iii + 118p.
     Unavailable for annotation.

24.  Bibliographic Information Bulletin on Integrated Develop-
     ment of Predominantly Rural Areas.  Prepared by the

U.N. Secretariat.  Dept. of Economic and Social Affairs.  Center for Social Development and Humanitar-
ian Affairs, Social Development Division, Institutional
Development and Popular Participation Section, 1976.
29p.
Unavailable for annotation.

25.  Bibliography on Rural and Community Development.
     Las Cruces:  Educational Resources Information Cen-
     ter, Clearinghouse on Rural Education and Small
     Schools, New Mexico State University, 1976.  61p.
     ED 135 550.
     This bibliography results from a computer search of
the ERIC files from January 1973 through December 1975 using the terms "rural development" and "community development."  Part I consists of reproductions from Resources in
Education; Part II of entries from Current Index to Journals
in Education.  Part III is a subject index providing an index
by major descriptors to each of the citations.  Part IV is a
directory of ERIC clearinghouses and order forms for the
ERIC Document Reproduction Service.

26.  Bista, Khem B.  Bibliography on Rural Development in
     Nepal.  Kathmandu, Nepal:  Development Research
     and Communication Group, 1981.  78 leaves.
     A wide range of published and unpublished items--
journal articles, government reports, unpublished research
papers, etc.--are listed in this bibliography.  The bibliography is not restricted by date of publication although most
citations are to material from the 1970's.
     Arrangement is by author within 25 subject chapters
that include "Local Administration," "Rural Health," "Rural
Industries," "Rural Social Structure," etc.  There are no
indexes.

27.  Bista, N., et al.  Integrated Rural Development:
     Country Profile; Inventory of Programmes, Institu-
     tions and Bibliography--Nepal.  CIRDAP Study Se-
     ries, no. 12.  Bangladesh:  Center on Integrated
     Rural Development for Asia and the Pacific, 1982.
     Unavailable for annotation.

28.  Bogale, M., and A. Temesgen.  Selected Bibliography
     of Materials Related to Ethiopia's Agricultural Devel-

opment. Addis Ababa: Imperial Ethiopian Government, 1971.
Unavailable for annotation.

29. Bokhari, A.S., and S. Maqsud. Integrated Rural Development: Country Profile; Inventory of Programmes, Institutions, and Bibliography--Pakistan.
CIRDAP Study Series, no. 13. Bangladesh: Center
on Integrated Rural Development for Asia and the
Pacific, 1982.
Unavailable for annotation.

30. Bollinger, Irene. Northern Development: People, Resources, Ecology and Transportation in the Yukon
and the Northwest Territories; A Bibliography of
Government Publications with Selected Annotations.
Exchange Bibliography, no. 643. Monticello, IL:
Council of Planning Librarians, 1974. 13p.
This bibliography presents a selected list of works
by or sponsored by government agencies. All titles were
published between the mid-1960's and 1973. A section on
general information sources is followed by four subject
chapters--people, resources, ecology, and transportation.
There are no indexes.

31. Bose, P.R., and V.N. Vashist. Rural Development and
Technology: A Status Report-cum-Bibliography.
New Delhi: Centre for the Study of Science, Technology, and Development, 1980. 373p.
This is an extensive bibliography of a wide range of
materials published in the 1970's on all aspects of rural development. The focus of the bibliography is India but material on other geographical areas is also included.
The bibliography is organized into 32 chapters each
of which is further sub-divided by specific subject. Chapters on social aspects of rural life include "Demography,"
"Migration," "Rural Changes and Modernization," "Rural Development," "Socio-Cultural Aspects," "Socio-economic Aspects," and "Village Development." Within chapters arrangement is alphabetical by author.
The bibliography concludes with an author index and
appendices on statistics, lists of journals and Indian newspapers covered in the bibliography, and a directory of Indian
institutions, organizations, and agencies engaged in rural
development.

32. Broadbent, K.P. Chinese Agriculture and Rural Society.
      Commonwealth Bureau of Agricultural Economics, An-
      notated Bibliography, no. 30. Commonwealth Agri-
      cultural Bureaux, 1974. 37p.
      Items in this bibliography were taken from World Ag-
ricultural Economics and Rural Sociology Abstracts between
1970 and 1973 and are arranged into several subject chapters,
e.g., "Agricultural Policy," "Communes and Co-operatives,"
and "Social Issues." There is a concluding subject index.

33. Broadbent, K.P. Development Aid and Agriculture.
      Annotated Bibliography, no. 12. Oxford: Common-
      wealth Bureau of Agricultural Economics, 1972. 47p.
      Entries in this bibliography were taken from World
Agricultural Economics and Rural Sociology Abstracts and
are organized under three headings: "General Aspects,"
"Food Aid," and "Technical Assistance to Agriculture."
Four appendices provide financial information on aid world-
wide. There is also a subject index.

34. Broadbent, K.P. The Green Revolution. Commonwealth
      Bureau of Agricultural Economics, Annotated Bibliog-
      raphy, no. 1. Commonwealth Agricultural Bureaux,
      1971, Revised ed. 1973. 35p.
      The revised edition of this bibliography lists CAB
citations and abstracts relating to both technical and social/
economic aspects of the green revolution. Arrangement is by
author within subject sections such as "Factors of Production,"
"Extension," etc., and within a section that provides a 1973
supplement. Indexes provide access by subject and geography.

35. Broadbent, K.P. Oil Exploration and Land: A Review
      of Selected Current Literature Relating to Industriali-
      zation and Rural Development, with Special Reference
      to the Oil Industry, and to the North Sea Area in
      Particular. Commonwealth Bureau of Agricultural
      Economics, Annotated Bibliography, no. 23. Common-
      wealth Agricultural Bureaux, 1974. 45p.
      The emphasis in this bibliography is on journal arti-
cles from the early 1970's, although some books and government reports are also included. Various concerns surrounding oil exploration and development are discussed--pollution,
esthetic damage, and disruption to rural society.
      After an opening general section the bibliography is

arranged by author within geographic region. There is a
separate section devoted to oil development in the North Sea.
There is a concluding list of journals scanned and a subject
index.

36. Broadbent, K.P. Papua New Guinea Development Prob-
    lems. Commonwealth Bureau of Agricultural Econom-
    ics, Annotated Bibliography, no. 26. Commonwealth
    Agricultural Bureaux, 1974. 9p.
    Items in this bibliography were taken from World Ag-
ricultural Economics and Rural Sociology Abstracts, 1967-1973
and emphasize issues related to rural development. The bibliography is arranged within subject headings such as "Labour
and Wages," "Cooperation," "Land Problems," etc. There is
a concluding subject index.

37. Broadbent, K.P., and E. Schinke. Centrally Planned
    Agriculture: China and USSR; A Compilation of Re-
    view Articles and Annotated Bibliography. Review
    Publication, no. 2. Commonwealth Agricultural
    Bureaux, 1972. i + 42p.
    The bulk of this work consists of two review articles
--"Two Decades of Social and Economic Development in Chinese Communist Agriculture 1949-1969" by K.P. Broadbent
and "The Organization and Planning of Soviet Agriculture"
by E. Schinke. Each is followed by a bibliography, not restricted by language, on the social, economic, and political
aspects of agricultural development in China and the USSR.

38. Burg, Nan C. Economic Development in Nonmetropolitan
    Areas: Special Socioeconomic Problems of Rapid-
    Growth Communities; A Select Bibliography. Ex-
    change Bibliography, no. 1497. Monticello, IL:
    Council of Planning Librarians, 1978. 24p.
    This bibliography includes federal and state govern-
ment documents, technical reports, books, articles, and conference proceedings published in the 1960's and 1970's. The
bibliography is organized into several sections: "Effect of
population shifts on nonmetropolitan areas," "Effect of economic development on the quality of life in nonmetropolitan
areas," "Impacts of community development programs on nonmetropolitan areas," "Specific economic development in nonmetropolitan areas," "Impact of economic development programs
by private business and industry on nonmetropolitan development," "Impact of government assistance and programs on

nonmetropolitan area economic development," "Special socio-
economic problems of rapid growth in nonmetropolitan areas,"
and "Sources and resources for additional information." The
last section lists bibliographies, periodicals, and organizations.
Within the other sections entries are listed alphabetically by
author. There are no indexes.

39. Burg, Nan C. Toward an Investment Strategy for Rural
    Economic Development in Pennsylvania: A Bibliogra-
    phy with Selected Annotations. Public Administration
    Series, no. P-96. Monticello, IL: Vance Bibliogra-
    phies, 1978. 32p.
    This bibliography is organized into several subject
sections: "The Planner's Role in Rural Economic Development," "Rural Economic Development, General," "Rural Economic Development, Specific," "Federal Role in Rural Economic Development," "Population Distribution and Redistribution,"
and "Useful Sources for Additional Information." Besides
books and journal articles, the author includes a variety of
reports from official and quasi-official agencies, most of which
were published in the 1970's. The bibliography is useful for
information on all of the United States, not just Pennsylvania.

40. Buzzard, Shirley. Rural Development Literature 1976-
    77: An Updated Annotated Bibliography. Columbia:
    Extension Division, University of Missouri, 1978.
    47p. ED 157 648.
    "More than 100 books and articles on rural develop-
ment published during 1976-77 are annotated in this selected
bibliography. Concentrating on social science literature, the
bibliography is interdisciplinary in nature, spanning agricultural economics, anthropology, community development, community health, and rural sociology." The bibliography is
limited to works dealing with the U.S. and is arranged in
one alphabetical list by author. There is a topic index with
31 categories.

41. Caballero, Lorenzo, and Katarina Carlqvist. Guinea-
    Bissau--A Bibliography Covering the Rural Sector
    with Emphasis on the Period After 1975. Working
    Paper, no. 21. Uppsala: International Rural De-
    velopment Centre, Swedish University of Agricul-
    tural Sciences, 1984. 31 leaves.
    "This bibliography records books, articles, project
documents and reports from international and national

organizations--in English, French, Portuguese as well as
Danish and Swedish--obtained from Swedish research librar-
ies. AGRIS and AGRICOLA have also been included."
Arrangement is by author within 14 subject divisions.
Citations provide bibliographic information as well as informa-
tion on the location of the items in Swedish institutions.
There is a concluding author index.

42. Carvajal, Manuel J. Economic and Rural Development in
    Central America and Panama, 1975-1980: A Bibliog-
    raphy. [Washington, D.C.]: U.S. Agency for In-
    ternational Development, 1982. 1270p.
    This bibliography is intended to supplement and ex-
    pand earlier A.I.D. bibliographies. A wide range of works
    is included. Some citations are annotated; each is coded to
    one or more broad subject areas and one or more types of
    publication, i.e., U.S. government publication; publication
    by a foreign government; publication by regional or interna-
    tional organization; book by commercial publisher; publication
    by nonprofit, nonuniversity organization; university publica-
    tion except thesis or dissertation; thesis or dissertation; ar-
    ticle or chapter within a book; or journal article.
    Arrangement is by author under country. There
    are concluding indexes by name, topic, geographical place,
    and institution.

43. Carvajal, Manuel J. Economic and Rural Development in
    the Caribbean, 1975-1980: A Bibliography. [Wash-
    ington, D.C.]: U.S. Agency for International De-
    velopment, 1982. 623p.
    This work is intended to supplement and expand
    earlier A.I.D. bibliographies and is identical in range and
    format to the author's bibliography on Economic and Rural
    Development in Central America and Panama, 1975-1980.

44. Chuenyane, Z. Managing Development Projects: A Se-
    lected, Annotated Bibliography. Annotated Bibliogra-
    phy, no. 5. [East Lansing]: Non-Formal Education
    Information Center, Michigan State University, 1981.
    22p.
    Unavailable for annotation.

45. Cigar, Norman. Agriculture and Rural Development in
    Egypt. Public Administration Series, no. P-851.
    Monticello, IL: Vance Bibliographies, 1981. 7p.
    Listing the "principal works on agriculture and rural

development" in Egypt since 1952, the bibliography includes
the subjects of "administration and politics, land reform,
agricultural production, planning and marketing." Works in
English and French are included.

46.  Cigar, Norman.  Agriculture and Rural Development in
     the Arabian Peninsula.  Public Administration Series,
     no. P-699.  Monticello, IL:  Vance Bibliographies,
     1981.  4p.
     "This bibliography presents the more significant
works on agriculture and rural development in the Arabian
peninsula with special emphasis on the most important country, Saudi Arabia.  Though most works deal with the contemporary period, some which provide a historical background
are also included."

47.  Cigar, Norman.  Agriculture and Rural Development in
     the Fertile Crescent:  Lebanon, Syria, Jordan and
     Iraq.  Public Administration Series, no. P-698.
     Monticello, IL:  Vance Bibliographies, 1981.  5p.
     Arranged by country and then by author, "this bib-
liography presents the more significant publications--both
monographs and periodical articles--on various aspects of
the rural sector since 1945."

48.  Cigar, Norman.  Agriculture and Rural Development in
     the Sudan.  Public Administration Series, no. P-700.
     Monticello, IL:  Vance Bibliographies, 1981.  4p.
     "This bibliography includes books and periodical
articles on various aspects of agriculture in the Sudan since
the mid-1950s including those dealing with rural organizations
and land tenure, livestock, and the much-studied 'Gezira
Scheme' which involves state/individual cooperation in the
development of an extensive cotton producing region."

49.  Cigar, Norman.  Agriculture and Rural Development in
     Tunisia.  Public Administration Series, no. P-850.
     Monticello, IL:  Vance Bibliographies, 1981.  7p.
     "This bibliography presents the principal monographs
and articles dealing with agriculture and related aspects of
rural development in Tunisia since its independence in 1956
...."  Both French and English language publications are
represented.

50.  Clay, Edward J.  A Select Bibliography on Agricultural

Economics and Rural Development with Special Reference to Bangladesh. BARC Agricultural Economics
and Rural Social Science Papers, no. 1. Dacca:
Bangladesh Agricultural Research Council, 1977.
xiv + 100p.
This bibliography includes books that were in print
in mid-1976, when the bibliography was being compiled, as
well as periodical articles and ephemeral reports and documents.
The bibliography is organized into a variety of subject chapters and sub-chapters within which articles and reports are listed separately from books, usually for Bangladesh and then for other less developed countries. There
are no indexes.

51. Clay, Edward J., and Mavis N. Clay. A Select Bibli-
    ography on Agricultural Economics and Rural Devel-
    opment, with Special Reference to Bangladesh.
    Supplement and Author Index. BARC Agricultural
    Economics and Rural Social Science Papers, no. 6.
    Dacca: Bangladesh Agricultural Research Council,
    1978. xiv + 138p.
This supplement continues the bibliography up to the
beginning of 1978. Almost 800 new items have been added;
just under half pertain to Bangladesh. Some changes have
been made in the classification scheme used in the original
volume. The supplement concludes with an author index to
both the supplement and the original work.

52. Cohen, John M., et al. Participation at the Local Level:
    A Working Bibliography. Rural Development Bibliog-
    raphy Series, no. 1. Ithaca, NY: Rural Develop-
    ment Committee, Center for International Studies,
    Cornell University, 1978. vi + 121p.
This is an extensive bibliography intended for rural
development workers concerned with local participation in the
development process. Periodical articles, books, conference
papers, and manuscripts, with a few exceptions dating from
1960 to 1977, are included. Also included are U.S. and
Canadian Ph.D. dissertations from 1970 to 1977.
An eight-page introduction precedes the bibliography.
The bibliography itself is organized into nine chapters:
"Participation and Development," "Local Organization," "Local
Leadership and Elites," "Political Participation," "Political
Factors Affecting Participation," "Social Factors Affecting

Participation," "Institutional Contexts of Participation," "Participation and Community Development," and two final chapters on French and Spanish sources of participation. These last two chapters include a review of the literature and a selected annotated bibliography. All entries appear only once and are not cross-referenced. There are no indexes.

53. Cohen, John M., and Mary Hebert. Rural Development
in Yemen: A Select Bibliography. Working Note,
no. 14. [Ithaca, NY]: Rural Development Committee, Yemen Research Program, Center for International
Studies, Cornell University, [1983]. vi + 32 leaves.
This bibliography was produced as part of a Cornell
University, A.I.D. sponsored, research project on "Local
Organizations, Participation and Development in the Yemen
Arab Republic." Monographs, journal articles, government
documents, UN documents, and dissertations and other unpublished papers are all included. Not all items included
deal directly with rural development. Most works cited are
in English; there is no restriction by date of publication.
Arrangement is by author in one alphabetical list with no
subject divisions. There are no indexes.

54. Colloquium on Method of Planning for Comprehensive
Regional Development. Annotated Bibliography.
Prepared by the United Nations Secretariat. [New
York: United Nations Centre for Regional Development (1976?)]. 59p.
Articles, government and UN documents, books, conference proceedings, and dissertations published in the 1960's
and early 1970's are included in this bibliography. All entries deal with regional development; many of them specifically with rural development. Arrangement is by author. There
are no subject divisions or indexes.

55. Commonwealth Bureau of Agricultural Economics. African
Agriculture and Rural Development. Vol. I, General;
Vol. II, North and Northeast Africa; Vol. III, East
Africa; Vol. IV, South and Central Africa; Vol. V,
West Africa. Annotated Bibliographies, nos. R1-R5,
Series B. Commonwealth Agricultural Bureaux, 1975.
Vol. I, 32p.; Vol. II, 29p.; Vol. III, 59p.; Vol. IV,
37p.; Vol. V, 70p.
Designed to update their 1971 bibliography of African

agriculture, "this series is based on abstracts published in
World Agricultural Economics and Rural Sociology Abstracts
during the period July 1971 to December 1974.
    "The general, introductory volume brings together
general material on African agriculture and rural development, and references which cover more than one country in
such a way as not to fall conveniently within the regional
grouping of the other volumes in the series. The material
is arranged by subject ... and within these subjects in alphabetical order by author."
    In subsequent volumes "the material is introduced
by general references on the area or those which cover more
than one country. The main part of the bibliography is arranged geographically, and alphabetically by author within
each section. At the end are author and subject indexes,
and a list of serial publications scanned."

56. Commonwealth Bureau of Agricultural Economics. As-
    pects of Agricultural Policy and Rural Development
    in Africa: An Annotated Bibliography. Edited by
    Margot Bellamy. Annotated Bibliographies, Series B.
    Vol. I, General; Vol. II, North and Northeast Africa;
    Vol. III, East Africa; Vol. IV, South and Central
    Africa; Vol. V, West Africa. Commonwealth Agricul-
    tural Bureaux, 1971. Vol. I, 28p.; Vol. II, 31p.;
    Vol. III, 45p.; Vol. IV, 37p.; Vol. V, 63p.
    Material included in this series appeared in World
Agricultural Economics and Rural Sociology Abstracts between 1964 and mid-1971. Arrangement is by author within
subject sections, e.g., "Land Tenure and Reform," "Trade,"
and "Rural Sociology," in the general volume and by country
in the last four volumes. There are no indexes.

57. Commonwealth Bureau of Agricultural Economics. Evalu-
    ation and Monitoring of Rural Development Projects.
    Annotated Bibliography, no. RDA1/R50. Common-
    wealth Agricultural Bureaux.
    Unavailable for annotation. Secondary sources indi-
cate that this bibliography covers CAB indexes for the period
1976-1982 and lists 217 citations.

58. Commonwealth Bureau of Agricultural Economics. Latin
    America: Agricultural Situation and Development;
    Central America (Belize, Costa Rica, El Salvador,
    Guatemala, Honduras, Mexico, Nicaragua, Panama).

Annotated Bibliography, no. RE10. Commonwealth
Agricultural Bureaux, 1980. 70p.
    Unavailable for annotation. Secondary sources indi-
cate that this bibliography covers CAB indexes for the period
1978-1980 and lists 229 citations.

59. Commonwealth Bureau of Agricultural Economics. Latin
    America: Agricultural Situation and Development (1978-
    1980). Latin America (General). Annotated Bibliogra-
    phy, no. RE8. Commonwealth Agricultural Bureaux,
    1980. 36p.
        Unavailable for annotation. Secondary sources indi-
cate that this bibliography covers CAB indexes for the period
1978-80 and lists 125 references.

60. Commonwealth Bureau of Agricultural Economics. Latin
    America: Agricultural Situation and Development;
    South America (Argentina, Bolivia, Brazil, Chile).
    Annotated Bibliography, no. RE9(1). Commonwealth
    Agricultural Bureaux, 1980. 93p.
        Unavailable for annotation. Secondary sources indi-
cate that this bibliography covers CAB indexes for the period
1978-80 and lists 374 references.

61. Commonwealth Bureau of Agricultural Economics. Latin
    America: Agricultural Situation and Development;
    South America (Colombia, Ecuador, French Guiana,
    Guyana, Paraguay, Peru, Surinam, Uruguay, Vene-
    zuela). Annotated Bibliography, no. RE9(2). Com-
    monwealth Agricultural Bureaux, 1980. pp. 94-160.
        Unavailable for annotation. Secondary sources indi-
cate that this bibliography covers CAB indexes for the period
1978-80 and lists 236 references.

62. Commonwealth Bureau of Agricultural Economics. Re-
    gional Planning and Rural Development. Annotated
    Bibliography, no. 35. Commonwealth Agricultural
    Bureaux, 1975. 32p.
        Items in this bibliography were taken from World
Agricultural Economics and Rural Sociology Abstracts from
January 1974 through March 1975. Arrangement is by author
within continent and country. There are subject and author
indexes.

63. Commonwealth Bureau of Agricultural Economics. Rural
    Development in Africa 1973-1980. Vol. I and II.

Annotated Bibliography, no. R49. Commonwealth
Agricultural Bureaux, 1981. 365 leaves.
The more than 1,100 citations and annotations in
this bibliography are the result of an on-line search of CAB
abstracts. There are no subject divisions within the bibliography; arrangement is determined by the date the items were
entered into the data base. There is a geographical index
at the end of each volume.

64.  Commonwealth Bureau of Agricultural Economics. Rural
     Development in Central America and the Caribbean.
     Annotated Bibliography, no. RDA 4. Commonwealth
     Agricultural Bureaux.
     Unavailable for annotation. Secondary sources indi-
cate that this bibliography covers CAB indexes for the period
1978-81 and lists 363 references.

65.  Commonwealth Bureau of Agricultural Economics. Rural
     Development in the Middle East. Annotated Bibliog-
     raphy, no. RDA3/53. Commonwealth Agricultural
     Bureaux.
     Unavailable for annotation. Secondary sources indi-
cate that this bibliography covers CAB indexes for the period
1978-81 and lists 385 references.

66.  Comprehensive Bibliography on Bolivia Agrarian Reform.
     Prepared by the LTC/CIDA Research Team in Bolivia.
     [Madison]: Land Tenure Center, University of Wis-
     consin, 1973. 26p.
     English and Spanish language publications are listed
by author in one alphabetical list. There is no restriction
by date. This bibliography is available at the Land Tenure
Center Library, University of Wisconsin, Madison.

67.  Cortese, Charles F., and Jane Archer Cortese. The
     Social Effects of Energy Boomtowns in the West: A
     Partially Annotated Bibliography. Exchange Bibliog-
     raphy, no. 1557. Monticello, IL: Council of Plan-
     ning Librarians, 1978. 30p.
     Approximately 200 titles are listed by author in this
selected bibliography. The compilers have limited selection
to those items, often unpublished and difficult to locate,
which concern contemporary accounts of the social effects of
energy boomtowns in western U.S. states. Included are
"reports, symposia, proceedings, environmental impact

statements, and journalistic accounts." Not all citations are
to sociological research. "Some reports are detailed statistical descriptions, some are ethnographies, some very impres-
sionistic personal accounts."

68. Creager, J.M. Agricultural Development and Small
    Farm Families: Annotated Bibliography. Interdis-
    ciplinary Communication Program of the Smithsonian
    Institution, vol. 3, no. 1 (1975).
    Unavailable for annotation.

69. Crush, J.S. The Post-Colonial Development of Botswana,
    Lesotho and Swaziland. Public Administration Series,
    no. P-138. Monticello, IL: Vance Bibliographies,
    1978. 12p.
    "Works listed are limited to those published in the
English language and include relevant journal articles, monographs, conference papers, books and unpublished theses.
General works incorporating all three countries are listed in
the first section; followed by studies specific to Botswana,
Lesotho and then Swaziland. References are listed alphabetically rather than chronologically within each section."

70. Dayao, Benefa M. Small Farm Development: A Prelim-
    inary Annotated Bibliography of South and Southeast
    Asian Literature Covering the Period 1970-1976. Asian
    Bibliography Series, no. 1. Laguna, Philippines:
    Agricultural Information Bank for Asia, 1977. iv +
    160 leaves.
    "This bibliography is designed as a guide to regional
problems facing small farms. It presents a socio-economic
review of aspects of agricultural production. Particular
emphasis is placed on adoption of new technology, co-operation
and credit."
    Partially annotated and including a wide range of
both published and unpublished material, the bibliography is
organized into several subject chapters relating to farming,
e.g., farm management, migration, and adoption of innovations. Within these chapters arrangement is alphabetical by
author. The bibliography concludes with a list of periodicals
referred to, an author index, and a subject index.

71. Dejene, Tekola, and Scott E. Smith. Experiences in
    Rural Development: A Selected, Annotated Bibliog-
    raphy of Planning, Implementing, and Evaluating

Rural Development in Africa. OLC Paper, no. 1.
Washington, D.C.: Overseas Liaison Committee,
American Council on Education, 1973. 48p.
The focus of this bibliography is on English and
French language books, periodical articles, and conference
papers written between 1968 and 1973. "The majority of the
entries deal with actual rural development projects and focus
on their planning, implementation, evaluation, and training
aspects, rather than with more general literature on the political, cultural, social, or anthropological aspects of rural
development or the technical material on the agricultural sciences." While geographical emphasis in the bibliography is
on Africa, for comparative purposes some literature concerning rural development in Asia and Latin America has been
included.
    The bibliography is organized into two major sections:
"Africa" and "Selected Rural Development Experience in
Other Developing Areas." These sections are further divided
into subject sub-sections, within which entries are arranged
alphabetically by author. There is an author and a subject
index.

72.  Development Academy of the Philippines. Rural Develop-
     ment Bibliography: Preliminary Listings of Philippine
     Materials, Theoretical Literature, Technical Reports,
     and International Case Studies. Compiled by the
     Rural Integration Team, Countryside Development
     Program, Development Academy of the Philippines.
     [Makati, Philippines]: Publications Center, Develop-
     ment Academy of the Philippines, 1976. 5 vols.
    This bibliography on rural development in the Phil-
ippines was compiled from holdings in sixty libraries within
the Philippines. From the 14,000 titles located, 6,000 were
chosen without limitation on publication date.
    "The materials included in this listing are books,
journal articles, mimeographed and typewritten manuscripts,
B.S., M.S., and Ph.D. theses, newspaper articles and technical reports from various government and private agencies
and institutions."
    The five volumes are arranged into 22 subject cate-
gories covering social, economic, agricultural, technological,
and environmental aspects of rural development. Within
categories arrangement is by author. The Philippine library
location is given for most items.
    Each volume contains a forward, guide to users,

guide to subject classification, code for current location of
materials, list of agencies, and list of journals, bulletins and
other materials. A comprehensive author index appears at
the end of each volume.

73. Développement Rural dans le Tiers-Monde; Bibliographie
    Sélective / Rural Development in the Third World;
    Selective Bibliography. Papers and Documents of
    the I.C.I., Series C, no. 11. Ottawa: Institute
    for International Co-operation, University of Ottawa,
    1977. xviii + 249p. + 4p.

    Prepared in conjunction with an annual colloquium of
the Institute for International Co-operation, this bibliography
is organized around the four discussion themes of the colloquium: agriculture, fisheries, forestry, and community services. "The latter includes material on such areas as education and communications in the rural milieu as well as community health services, rural water supplies, etc. To this
were added two sections: the administration and evaluation
of rural development projects and the woman and rural development. Finally a chapter on Canadian policy for rural
development was compiled." The bibliography also has a
chapter on general works and a lengthy section arranged by
continent or country. It concludes with an appendix of other
bibliographies.

    "Publications in the French, English, and Spanish
languages have been included. The types of materials re-
searched were: monographs, periodicals, official documents
of francophone Africa, of the United Nations, and of international institutions, some Canadian and American official
publications, as well as the publications of the World Bank
and various international development banks." There is an
author index.

74. Dew, Ian F. A Selected Annotated Bibliography of Rural
    Canada / Bibliographie Annotée de Canada Rural.
    Ottawa: Central Mortgage and Housing Corp., 1976.
    ix + 434p.

    "This bibliography lists works of research and infor-
mation about rural areas and small communities in Canada
south of the Yukon and Northwest Territories. Its focus is
socio-economic development and planning, rather than history
and description.

    "This bibliography consists of 1,800 entries, divided
into eight main subject groups. Each subject group is

preceded by a note on the material included.  The entries
are arranged alphabetically by author within each group and
are indexed by subject, place, author, title, and series.
"A wide range of published documents is included:
monographs, journal articles, academic theses (master's and
doctoral), periodicals, and documents produced by all levels
of government.  The bibliography does not include newspaper articles, atlases, community directories (telephone and
business), promotional literature, or very detailed technical
reports; nor does it list documents published by Statistics
Canada."

75.  Dimit, Robert, et al.  Community Organization:  Urban
     and Rural Planning and Development.  Exchange
     Bibliography, no. 884.  Monticello, IL:  Council of
     Planning Librarians, 1975.  31p.
     "This bibliography which contains almost 500 sources
is geared for planners, academicians, researchers and other
interested parties.  The list contains books, monographs, and
journal articles dealing with planning, power, development,
and other aspects of community life."  Items on rural planning are scattered throughout the bibliography, which is organized into several subject categories, such as community
development, community planning, community studies, and
community organization.  Entries date from 1899 and are arranged by author within the subject divisions.  There are
no indexes.

76.  Eicher, Carl K.  Research on Agricultural Development
     in Five English-Speaking Countries in West Africa.
     New York:  Agricultural Development Council, 1970.
     153p.
     Four introductory chapters discuss rural development
problems and research in the five English-speaking nations
of West Africa.  Most of the book is devoted to an appendix/
bibliography that lists, with few exceptions, only works published between 1950 and 1969.
     The bibliography is organized into a section on West
Africa and then on each of the five nations.  Within these
sections arrangement is by type of material (e.g., bibliographies, books, government documents, journal articles, Ph.D.
dissertations, research in progress, unpublished papers) and
then by author.  Eicher also provides each entry with a number or numbers indicating the subject as revealed in a classification scheme presented at the end of the bibliography.
There are no other indexes.

77. Eicher, Shirley Fischer. Rural Development in Botswana:
    A Select Bibliography, 1966-1980. Washington, D.C.:
    African Bibliographic Center, 1981. iii + 145p.
    Partially annotated, this bibliography is organized
into seventeen subject chapters, most of which are concerned
with social aspects of rural development in Botswana. Included in the bibliography are U.S. and Botswana government documents, UN documents, periodical articles, papers,
theses, dissertations, and unpublished reports, almost all
of which date from the 1970's.
    Arrangement is alphabetical by author within chap-
ters. There is an author index.

78. Emery, Sarah Snell. Mexico's Rural Development and
    Education: A Select Bibliography. Public Adminis-
    tration Series, no. P-97. Monticello, IL: Vance
    Bibliographies, 1978. 33p.
    Both English and Spanish language publications are
included in this bibliography. "Since the problems faced by
the indigenous and rural communities and by those trying to
aid in their development are so varied, the first part of the
bibliography is on works illustrating the range of impediments
to rural development, as well as the attempted improvements.
The second half is on education, formal and informal, of
children and adults, as the best hope for increasing agricultural productivity without contributing to the pressures
toward urbanization. The research is nearly all post-1958."
    Official publications of the Mexican government have
been emphasized in the bibliography but books, articles, dissertations, etc. are also included.

79. Erickson, Frank A. An Annotated Bibliography of Agri-
    cultural Development in Jamaica. Jamaica, Working
    Document Series. [Washington, D.C.]: Rural De-
    velopment Division, Bureau for Latin America and
    the Caribbean, [U.S.] Agency for International De-
    velopment, 1979. 197p.
    While some of this bibliography is devoted to econom-
ic, technical, and environmental aspects of agriculture, chapters titled, "Agriculture: Socio-Economic Characteristics,
Overviews" and "Agriculture: Extension, Education, Organization" list a wide range of sociological studies. Most works
included were published in the 1960's or 1970's. There are
no indexes.

80. Ferguson, Donald S. A Conceptual Framework for the
    Evaluation of Livestock Production Development Proj-
    ects and Programs in Sub-Saharan West Africa with
    a Selected Bibliography of West African Livestock
    Development Compiled by Donald S. Ferguson and
    Jonathan Sleeper. [Ann Arbor]: Center for Re-
    search on Economic Development, University of Mich-
    igan [1977?].

    The 50-page bibliographic section of this work was
    compiled in 1976 and "is designed to assist persons initiating
    studies, project designs or project appraisals related to live-
    stock sector or rural development in West Africa." Partially
    annotated, it includes journal articles, monographs, govern-
    ment documents, and published and unpublished research
    papers. Both French and English language publications are
    included. Arrangement is alphabetical by author. There
    are no indexes.

81. Flower, Clara K. The Green Revolution. Readers Ad-
    visory Service. Selected Topical Booklist, no. 110
    (1975). 4p.

    This bibliography lists books and periodical articles,
    primarily from the late 1960's and early 1970's. There are
    three sections: books, periodicals available in the Fogler
    Library of the University of Maine, and periodical articles
    not available in the Fogler Library. Arrangement of books
    is by author; of periodical articles by title of journal.

82. Food and Agriculture Organization of the United Nations.
    A Record of Experience:  Catalogue of FFHC/Action
    for Development Documents, 1971-1976. Rome:  FAO,
    1977. x + 99p.

    Reports of FFHC/AD-sponsored development projects
    are annotated and arranged by region and country. There
    is a subject index.

83. Frankena, Frederick, and Thomas Kobernick. Commu-
    nity Impacts of Rapid Growth in Non-Metropolitan
    Areas; A Cross-Disciplinary Bibliography. Public
    Administration Series, no. P-560. Monticello, IL:
    Vance Bibliographies, 1980. 27p.

    251 published and unpublished items, primarily dat-
    ing from the 1970's and concerning rapid growth in U.S.
    non-metropolitan communities, are arranged in one alphabeti-

cal list by author. The bibliography ends with a classified
subject index providing access under the headings "Boomtowns and rapid development," "Controlling, managing, planning growth," "Rural industrialization," etc.

84.  Fredericks, L.J., and S. Nair. Integrated Rural De-
     velopment: Country Profile; Inventory of Pro-
     grammes, Institutions and Bibliography--Malaysia.
     CIRDAP Study Series, no. 11. Bangladesh:
     CIRDAP, 1982.
     Unavailable for annotation.

85.  French, David. Appropriate Technology in Social Con-
     text: An Annotated Bibliography. Mt. Rainier, MD:
     Volunteers in Technical Assistance, 1977. 33p.
     The majority of citations in this bibliography are to
works with a rural or village setting. Works cited are not
limited by date of publication although most of them were
published in the 1970's and include monographs, journal articles, government and UN publications, as well as unpublished reports of institutes and organizations. All concern
social effects of technological innovation. Arrangement is
alphabetical by author with no sub-divisions or indexes.

86.  Fukui, Hayao; Hiroshi Tsujii; and Masuo Kuchiba.
     A Bibliography on Rural Development in Monsoon
     Asia. Information Service, no. 18. [Bangkok]:
     Association of Development Research and Training
     Institutes of Asia and the Pacific, 1977. 194p.
     This is an extensive bibliography of a wide range of
works in English relating to rural development in Asia. The
bibliography is not limited by date of publication and is organized into subject chapters and sub-chapters--e.g., economic aspects, sociocultural aspects, agriculture, etc.--
within which arrangement is by country and author. There
is an author index.

87.  Gabriel, Tom. Understanding the Local Social Condi-
     tions in Extension Training: A Guide to Literature.
     [Reading, U.K.: Agricultural Extension and Rural
     Development Centre, University of Reading], 1980.
     iii + 49p.
     Most of this work is devoted to a bibliography in-
tended to introduce extension trainees to anthropological literature relevant to the process of social change. Rural
areas are emphasized.

Most citations are to works published in journals or books. A few citations to films are included. Arrangement is by author within subject sections that include: "Anthropology and Development," "Agriculture, Innovation, and Economic Development," "Roles of Women," "Health, Medicine and Nutrition," "Population Issues," "Education," "Tourism," and "Data Collection." There are no indexes.

88. Gellar, Sheldon. Development by and for the People: A Select Annotated Bibliographical Guide to Participatory Development Issues. [Paris]: Organization for Economic Cooperation and Development, 1982. i + 75p.

"The bibliography is divided into five main components or sections. The first section presents a wide range of approaches towards participation and discusses different concepts, theories, and methodologies to be found in the participation literature.... The second section focuses on planning and management issues. Its entries reflect an essentially top-down, managerial perspective towards participatory rural development, the kind likely to be held by planners, government officials, and private agencies concerned with working effectively with local populations. In contrast, the third section looks at participation primarily from the bottom-up or grassroots perspective. Entries in this section describe and analyze different forms of participation--animation rurale, community development, and cooperatives--as well as the different groups identified as the main targets of participatory development projects--the poor, small farmers, women, etc. The fourth section deals exclusively with participatory development issues and case studies drawn from Sahelian West African experiences. Finally, the fifth section provides a resource guide to enable the reader to delve further into the subject. Hence it includes a list of bibliographies, journals, and periodicals to which the reader can turn for further information. It also describes more than sixty institutes, agencies, and groups involved in participatory development research and/or action-oriented programs."

A wide range of French and English language publications, primarily published in the 1970's and early 1980's is included. There are concluding author and geographical indexes.

89. Gorman, Lyn. Bibliography on Community and Rural Development: Europe, 1978-81. Langhold, Dum-

friesshire, [Scotland]: Arkleton Trust, 1982, iii +
251p.
"This bibliography attempts to provide comprehensive
coverage of the literature on community and rural development in Europe for the period 1978-81 inclusive. Some earlier materials have also been included, although complete coverage of any pre-1978 publications has not been attempted....
The material is presented in classified order, listed alphabetically by author within each section. Cross references
are provided at the beginning of each section."
Citations and annotations in the bibliography were
selected from World Agricultural Economics and Rural Sociology Abstracts and refer to works in English and several
other languages. Subject and geographical indexes are provided.

90.  Graber, Eric S.  An Annotated Bibliography of Rural
     Development and Levels of Living in Guatemala.
     Guatemala, General Working Document, no. 1.
     [Washington, D.C.]: Rural Development Division,
     Bureau for Latin America and the Caribbean, [U.S.]
     Agency for International Development, 1979.  81p.
     "This bibliography concerns rural development and
general living conditions in Guatemala. Included are publications and reports in the disciplines of economics, sociology,
anthropology, political science, agriculture, nutrition, and
history." Works in English or Spanish published since 1955
are included.
     The bibliography is arranged in one alphabetical list
by author. There are no indexes but "bibliographical entries
have been classified according to four subject matter areas
as follows: "(1) general development, social conditions and
levels of living; (2) agriculture; (3) rural life and organization; and (4) small farm development, technology and marketing." These subjects have been sub-divided to form a total
of 21 categories. Each entry has been assigned one or more
category abbreviations.

91.  Graber, Eric S.  An Annotated Bibliography of Rural
     Development, Urbanization, and Levels of Living in
     Peru.  Peru, General Working Document, no. 1.
     [Washington, D.C.]: Rural Development Division,
     Bureau for Latin America and the Caribbean, [U.S.]
     Agency for International Development, 1979.  109p.
     "This bibliography concerns rural development and

general living conditions in Peru. Included are publications and reports in the disciplines of economics, sociology, anthropology, political science, agriculture, nutrition, and history." Works in English or Spanish published after 1950 are included. The bibliography is arranged in one alphabetical list by author. There are no indexes but "bibliographical entries have been classified according to four subject matter areas as follows: (1) general development, social conditions and level of living; (2) agriculture; (3) rural life and organization; and (4) small farm development, technology and marketing." These subjects have been sub-divided to form a total of 21 categories. Each entry has been assigned one or more category abbreviations.

92. Hailu, Alem Seged. Rural Development in African Countries: A Selected Bibliography with Special Reference to Mali and Kenya. Public Administration Series, no. P-908. Monticello, IL: Vance Bibliographies, 1982. 29p.
The emphasis in this annotated, multidisciplinary bibliography is on journal articles and monographs published in the 1970's. Arrangement is alphabetical by author. There are no subject divisions or indexes.

93. Haque, Serajul; Shamsul Islam Khan; and Nilufar Akhter. Green Revolution: A Select Bibliography (1950 to 1977). BIDS Library Bibliography Series, no. 5. Dacca: Bangladesh Institute of Development Studies, 1978. 42p.
Materials listed in this bibliography are available in the Bangladesh Institute of Development Studies Library and include "research reports, working papers, seminar papers, discussion papers, periodical articles, reprint articles, documents and 'work in progress' type of material published in the field of economics and other social sciences."
There is an emphasis on works on Bangladesh although some works on the green revolution in other countries are also included. Arrangement is alphabetical by author. There are no indexes.

94. Harrington, Clifford R. Community Resource Development: A Preliminary Bibliography of Extension-Related Material in the Northeast. Ithaca, NY: Northeast Regional Center for Rural Development, Cornell University, 1973. 11p.

This bibliography lists by author, within each of the twelve northeastern states, the extension publications from those states that concern community development/rural development programs.

95.  Hirtz, Frank.  Bibliography on the Philippine Agrarian Reform and Related Areas.  Manila:  Food and Agriculture Organization, U.N., 1981.  iii leaves + 107p.  Unavailable for annotation.

96.  Högblom, Göran.  Botswana.  Uppsala:  Rural Development Section, Agricultural College of Sweden, 1973.  iv + 42 leaves.
While a wide range of materials is included in this bibliography, the emphasis is on government and UN documents and technical reports published between 1967 and 1972.  The bibliography is organized into four chapters:  "Natural resources," "Agriculture and agricultural development," "Socio-economic situation and development planning," and "Rural development."  Within chapters or sub-chapters arrangement is alphabetical by author.  There are no cross-references or indexes.

97.  Hoggart, Keith.  Rural Development:  A Bibliography.  Public Administration Series, no. 789.  2 vols.  Monticello, IL:  Vance Bibliographies, 1981.  276p.
This is an extensive bibliography which the compiler states is biased toward his own interests and "oriented towards geographic interpretations of rural development in Western Nations."  The two volumes are arranged in one consecutive list by author.  There is both a subject and a geographical index.  Studies concerning Britain, Canada, or the U.S. are most heavily represented in the 3,087 citations.

98.  Holdcroft, L.E.  The Rise and Fall of Community Development in Developing Countries, 1950-65:  A Critical Analysis and an Annotated Bibliography.  MSU Rural Development Paper, no. 2.  East Lansing:  Dept. of Agricultural Economics, Michigan State University, 1978.  iii + 72p.
The first sections of this work present a narrative description of the community development movement of the 1950's and 1960's and the implications of those experiences for rural development programs of the 1970's and 1980's.  The last two sections present a selected literature review

and bibliography of important monographs, journal articles,
and reports on community development from the 1950's and
1960's.

99. Horowitz, Michael M., and John Van Dusen Lewis.
    The Sociology and Political Economy of the Sahel:
    An Annotated Bibliography. Binghamton, NY:
    Institute for Development Anthropology, 1979.
    "This bibliography is prepared as a guide, to as-
    sist (AID) development officers and contract personnel in
    the identification, design, implementation and assessment of
    socially sound programs and projects which both benefit
    rural low income populations in the Sahel and are based on
    their needs, interests, and participation. It is not compre-
    hensive. It emphasizes monographic material...."
    The bibliography includes both French and English
    language publications and is not limited by date, although
    there is an emphasis on works published in the 1970's. Ar-
    rangement is by country and author. There are no indexes.

100. Hoskins, Myrna S., et al. A Synthesis of Evaluative
     Research Literature for Rural Development in the
     Southern Region: A Preliminary Bibliography.
     Departmental Information Report, no. 76-4. College
     Station: Dept. of Rural Sociology, Texas A & M
     University, 1976. ii + 59 leaves. ED 129 522.
     This bibliography is divided into six subject chap-
     ters, two of which are further sub-divided. The subject
     divisions are: "Major Sources," "Definitions of Rural De-
     velopment," "Definitions of Evaluation," "Criteria-Setting,"
     "Strategies of Evaluation--Methodology," "Strategies of
     Evaluation--Case Studies," "Evaluative Research and Evalu-
     ator's Responsibilities," and "Research in Progress." Within
     each of these categories books, periodical articles, govern-
     ment documents, and unpublished reports and papers are ar-
     ranged alphabetically by author. Although the bibliography
     is not limited by date of publication, most citations are to
     works published in the 1960's or 1970's. There are no in-
     dexes.

101. Ichimura, Shin'ichi, and Hiroshi Tsujii. A Preliminary
     Bibliography on Rural Development and Technologi-
     cal Innovations in Asia. Asian Association of Devel-
     opment Research and Training Institutes, 1976. 76p.
     Books, periodical articles, conference proceedings,

unpublished papers, U.S. government documents, dissertations, and theses are arranged in one list by author. There
are no subject divisions and no indexes. Most entries date
from 1960. The compilers have broadly defined the subject
areas of rural development and technology transfer within
agriculture.

102. Integrated Rural Development: Country Profile; In-
     ventory of Programmes, Institutions and Bibliography
     --India. CIRDAP Study Series, no. 10, 1982.
     Unavailable for annotation.

103. Jameson, Kenneth. An Annotated Bibliography of
     Agricultural Development in Guyana. [Guyana]
     Working Document, no. 1. [Washington, D.C.]:
     Development Studies Program, U.S. Agency for
     International Development, 1977.
     The 190 items in this bibliography include mono-
graphs, journal articles, theses, dissertations, government
documents, etc. and are arranged in one list by author.
There are no indexes but nine subject categories were developed and abbreviations next to each entry indicate in
which category or categories the work belongs. Works
written post-independence are emphasized.

104. Jones, E.A. Agriculture and Industry in Economic
     Development. Commonwealth Bureau of Agricultural
     Economics, Annotated Bibliography, no. 18. Com-
     monwealth Agricultural Bureaux, 1973. 16p.
     Most of the 104 references included in this bibliog-
raphy were taken from World Agricultural Economics and
Rural Sociology Abstracts, 1971-1973. There is a brief addendum of additional material. The bibliography is arranged
by author within continent and country. There are no indexes.

105. Khan, A.A. Integrated Rural Development: Country
     Profile; Inventory of Programmes, Institutions and
     Bibliography--Bangladesh. CIRDAP Study Series,
     no. 9, 1982.
     Unavailable for annotation.

106. Khoo, Siew Mun. A Bibliography on Rural Development
     in Southeast Asia. Kuala Lumpur: Library, Faculty
     of Economics and Administration, University of
     Malaya, 1974. 60p.

    All of the works cited in this bibliography are lo-
cated in the Library of the Faculty of Economics and Administration, University of Malaya, with the exception of theses
and dissertations which the compiler identified by consulting
other reference sources. Books, UN documents, government
documents, etc. are included but periodical articles are not.
The bibliography is arranged by subject and author and not
restricted by date of publication. There are no indexes.

107. Kocher, James E., and Beverly Fleischer. A Bibliog-
      raphy on Rural Development in Tanzania. MSU Rural
      Development Paper, no. 3. East Lansing: Dept. of
      Agricultural Economics, Michigan State University,
      1979. 77p. ED 171 495.
    English language publications from the late 1960's
through the late 1970's are the focus of this bibliography.
Included in the bibliography are journal articles, books, and
government documents as well as dissertations, theses, and
other unpublished papers. The bibliography is organized
into 28 chapters on specific aspects of rural development,
e.g., land tenure, rural co-operatives, women in rural development, etc. Within chapters arrangement is alphabetical
by author. There is an author index. Kocher's earlier,
shorter bibliography with the same title was published by
the Harvard Institute for International Development as the
Development Discussion Paper, no. 30, June 1977.

108. Kostinko, Gail, and Josué Dioné. An Annotated Bibli-
      ography of Rural Development in Senegal; 1975-1980.
      African Rural Economy Paper, no. 23. East Lansing:
      African Rural Economy Program, Dept. of Agricul-
      tural Economics, Michigan State University, 1980.
      73p.
    French and English language books, journal articles,
research papers, UN and government documents, theses and
dissertations are listed in this bibliography dealing exclusively with Senegal. Materials covering a larger geographical unit
are included only if they include a chapter or section on
Senegal. Since the bibliography was compiled in the United
States, many Senegalese government publications were not
available for annotation and were thus not included in the
bibliography.
    The bibliography is organized into a variety of sub-
ject chapters and sub-chapters within which arrangement is
alphabetical by author. There is an author index.

109. Kuchiba, Masao.  A Second Bibliography on Rural De-
     velopment and Technological Innovations in Asia.  A
     Supplement on Malaysia.  [Kyoto, Japan]:  Associa-
     tion of Development Research and Training, Insti-
     tutes of Asia and the Pacific, 1976.  41p.
     Theses, dissertations, books, periodical articles,
conference papers, unpublished papers, and government
documents are listed by author in this bibliography on Malaysia.  Citations are primarily to items published in the
1960's through early 1970's.  There are no indexes.

110. Kuennen, Daniel S.  Current Research and Periodicals
     on Rural Development, 1968-1971.  Georgetown:
     Cooperative Extension Service, University of Dela-
     ware, 1973.
     Unavailable for annotation.

111. Little, Peter D.  The Socio-economic Aspects of Pas-
     toralism and Livestock Development in Eastern and
     Southern Africa:  An Annotated Bibliography.
     Land Tenure Center Special Bibliography.  [Madi-
     son:  Land Tenure Center, University of Wiscon-
     sin], 1980.  38p.
     Unavailable for annotation.

112. Lund, K.T., and Nate Lund.  A Bibliography of
     Communities and Rapid Growth:  Information in the
     Leslie J. Savage Library.  Gunnison, CO:  Western
     Colorado Rural Communities Institute, Western State
     College, 1979.  iv + 36p.
     This is a selected and annotated bibliography de-
signed to provide citations to recent, relevant, and practical
information.  There is a strong emphasis on Colorado.
     Arrangement is by author within seven subject sec-
tions, each of which has three or four sub-sections.  The
seven subject sections are:  "Rapid Growth Situations,"
"Basic Information Sources," "The Planning Process," "Financing Growth," "Land Use Planning," "Planning for Water
and Waste," and "Planning for the Social Environment."
There are no indexes.

113. MacDonald, Allan F., and Harold J. O'Connell.
     Selected Annotated Bibliography of Recent Research
     on Rural Life on Prince Edward Island.  P.E.I.
     Community Studies, Report, no. 1.  Charlottetown:

Dept. of Sociology and Anthropology, Prince Edward
Island University, 1972.  75p.  ED 080 262.

This is a list of approximately 80 research reports
completed between the late 1960's and early 1970's that are
relevant to rural life and rural development on Prince Edward Island.  Arrangement is alphabetical by author within
four subject divisions:  "Agriculture-Fisheries-Tourism,"
"Business-Economics-Finance," "Development and Planning,"
and "Education-Health-Welfare."  An appendix gives background information on the four major research programs on
the Island that generated the majority of the citations listed
in the bibliography.

114.  McGrath, Mary Jean.  "Abstracts from Recent Litera-
      ture on Cooperatives, Small Farmers, and Develop-
      ment," in Cooperatives, Small Farmers & Rural De-
      velopment, 69-132.  Madison:  University Center
      for Cooperatives, University of Wisconsin-Extension,
      1978.

Extensively annotated, this bibliography lists journal articles, government and UN reports, unpublished research, conference proceedings, etc. that concern agricultural cooperatives and rural development.  There is no geographical restriction.  Arrangement is alphabetical by author.
There are no indexes.

115.  Mishra, Madhu S.  Bibliography on Management of
      Rural Development.  Calcutta:  Publications Divi-
      sion, Indian Institute of Management.  Vol. 1, 1983.
      320p.

"There are 3400 entries in this volume which include
books, government publications, reports and articles published in periodicals as well as composite books.  These have
been broadly divided into two groups (a) Books and (b) Articles.  Under each group, entries are arranged [by title]
under specific subject headings such as administration, ani-
mal husbandry, agriculture, employment, education...."
Indian publications and issues concerning rural development in India are emphasized.  The bibliography is not
restricted by date of publication although most items included
are from 1970 through the early 1980's.  There is an author
index.

116.  MPCRD Research Team.  A Bibliography on Local Level
      Planning.  Nagoya, Japan:  United Nations Centre
      for Regional Development, [1980?].  25 leaves.

This bibliography is organized into the following
main sections: "Basic Needs: Concepts, Measurement and
Policies," "Village Studies: Microlevel Planning," and "Rural
Development." Each of these is further divided into sections
on "Books and pamphlets," "Periodical articles," and "Meeting Papers and Proceedings." Most citations are to works
from the 1970's. There is no geographical focus or limitation.

117.  National Institute of Community Development. Green
      Revolution; A Select Bibliography. Hyderabad,
      [India]:  The Institute, 1972.  19p.
      Unavailable for annotation.

118.  Nwanosike, Eugene O.  Integrated Rural Development:
      A Select Bibliography (Part One).  Regional PAID-
      WA Bibliographical Series, no. 9.  Buea, Cameroon:
      Regional Pan African Institute for Development,
      1980.  12p.
      This is a listing by author of relevant material in
the library of the Regional Pan African Institute for Development in Buea.  Primarily listed are journal articles and unpublished papers from the 1970's.  Works on Africa are emphasized.

119.  Nwanosike, Eugene O.  Popular Participation and Rural
      Development in Africa:  A Select Annotated Bibliog-
      raphy.  Regional PAID-WA Bibliographical Series,
      no. 16.  Buea, Cameroon:  Regional Pan African
      Institute for Development, 1982.  27 leaves.
      Compiled for a Pan African Institute for Develop-
ment seminar on "Development and People's Participation in
Africa" held in 1983, this bibliography lists relevant English
language publications available in the PAID-WA library.  Arrangement is by author.  Citations are to a variety of published and unpublished works, mostly dating from the late
1970's and early 1980's.  Africa is emphasized.

120.  Nwanosike, Eugene O.  Power Relations & Poverty in
      Rural Development:  A Preliminary Bibliography.
      Regional PAID-WA Bibliographical Series, no. 15.
      Buea, Cameroon:  Regional Pan African Institute
      for Development, 1982.  19p. + 2p.
      This bibliography was compiled for participants in a
workshop on "Power Relations and Poverty in Rural Develop-

ment" held in Buea in 1982. Citations are to works in the
Regional PAID Library, are annotated, and are arranged in
one alphabetical list by author. There is an addendum of
unannotated citations to works in French. Works on Africa
are emphasized.

121. Nwanosike, Eugene O. Primary Health Care and Rural
     Development: A Select Annotated Bibliography.
     Regional PAID-WA Bibliographical Series, no. 17.
     Buea, Cameroon: Regional Pan African Institute
     for Development, 1983. 32p.
     Developed for a short course for African paramedi-
cal students, this bibliography lists publications in the library of PAID-WA. The first part of the bibliography lists
"documents, reports, and articles." The second part lists
"PAID/WA student case studies on various aspects of primary
health care." Arrangement is by author within each of
these sections. Works in the first section are not restricted
to Africa; works in the second section are.

122. Nwanosike, Eugene O. Role and Problems of Self-Help
     Organizations/Institutions in Rural Development: A
     Select Bibliography of Documents Found in Buea
     RPAID Library (Part One). [Regional PAID-WA
     Bibliographical Series, no. 3?] Buea, Cameroon:
     Regional Pan African Institute for Development,
     1979. 6p.
     This brief bibliography lists relevant material by
author. The emphasis is on books and journal articles from
the 1960's and early 1970's although some UN and government publications are also included. There is no geographical emphasis.

123. Nwanosike, Eugene O. Women and Rural Development:
     A Select and Partially Annotated Bibliography. Re-
     gional PAID-WA Bibliographical Series, no. 10.
     Buea, Cameroon: Regional Pan African Institute
     for Development, [1982?]. 63p.
     Books; journal articles; conference proceedings;
and reports of governments, the UN, and various commissions are all included in this bibliography. Items listed
were drawn from the library of the Regional Pan African
Institute for Development. Most were published in the
1970's or 1980's. There is no geographical limitation.
     The bibliography is organized by author within

subject chapters that include general studies, education and
training, women and rural development, etc. There are no
indexes.

124.  O'Keefe, Liz, and Michael Howes.  "A Select Annotated
      Bibliography: Indigenous Technical Knowledge in
      Development," IDS Bulletin 10, no. 2 (1979):51-58.
Published and unpublished research papers, journal
articles, and monographs, primarily from the 1970's and concerning indigenous technical knowledge in agriculture are
listed in this bibliography.

125.  Onuorah, Regina.  Community Development Projects
      Linked with Agricultural Settlement Schemes:  A
      Selected Bibliography.  Ibadan:  Nigerian Institute
      of Social and Economic Research, University of
      Ibadan, 1974.  16p.
This bibliography covers the subjects of "1. Community development projects linked with agricultural settlement schemes with a technical assistance component aimed at
agricultural training and information management of agricultural co-operatives and marketing.  2. The evaluation of
such projects with a view to identifying possible pitfalls and
solutions thereto, and improving the development planning
function (inclusive of development planning research).
      "The list covers books, periodical articles, newspa-
per cuttings, conference reports and research findings both
on Nigerian farm settlements and a few other countries."
Arrangement is by author under subject divisions such as
"Communications," "Co-operation," "Agricultural Extension--
Evaluation," etc.

126.  Opubor, Alfred E., and Mary Kay Hobbs.  "Develop-
      ment Communications:  A Selective Annotated Bib-
      liography," Rural Africana 27 (Spring 1975):127-156.
      This bibliography "annotates selected materials re-
lated to the broad domain of communication and information
diffusion in rural Africa:  the majority of items fall within
the areas of communication, education, and agriculture.
Pertinent studies from other countries having theoretical or
applicative value to development communications in Africa
are indicated by an asterisk."  Arrangement is by author
under headings denoting type of material--bibliographies,
books, monographs and published reports, etc.  Most citations are to works published between the mid-1960's and
the mid-1970's.

127. Parker, Carrie G.; Howard W. Ladewig; and Edward L.
     McLean. A Bibliography of Rural Development:
     Listings by Topic. AE, no. 391. Clemson, SC:
     Dept. of Agricultural Economics and Rural Sociology.
     Clemson University, 1976. 80p. ED 127 100.
     Nineteen journals relevant to the field of rural de-
velopment were indexed to form this bibliography. The volumes indexed date from 1950 to 1975. The bibliography is
organized by topic and sub-topic. Topics include agriculture, area development, community, economic development,
environmental improvement, facilities and services, human
resource development, leadership, organization, rural development, rural-urban relationships, and social action.
Within sub-topics entries are arranged by author. Entries
are sometimes listed more than once and are cross-referenced.
There are no indexes.

128. Pathak, Angelika. Landwirtschaftliche Entwicklung in
     Südasien (Auswahlbibliographie) / A Select Bibliog-
     raphy on Agricultural Development in South Asia.
     Dokumentationsdienst Asien, Series A, no. 11.
     Hamburg: Institute of Asian Affairs, Asia Docu-
     mentation Center, 1978. xxviii + 208p.
     Entries in this bibliography are photocopies of cata-
log cards from the Asia Documentation Center. While subject
headings are in German, most of the works included are in
English. "Included are primarily monographs but also official
publications and articles as far as these are entered in the
catalogues of the Asia Documentation Center.... Usually material published within the last 10-12 years was selected but
in the case of smaller countries older monographs were included as well.... The material was classified first along
geographical, then thematic, finally chronological lines. The
region South Asia is followed by the countries Bangladesh,
Nepal, Sri Lanka and India.... Within each section, the material is ordered according to date of publication, such that
the latest comes first. The bibliography lists 1,238 titles,
out of which 10 are on South Asia, 68 on Bangladesh, 78 on
Sri Lanka, 23 on Nepal and 1,063 on India."

129. Perkins, Lee Ann. A Selected Bibliography on Rural
     Development in Socialist Countries. [New York]:
     Ford Foundation, 1973. 55 leaves.
     "This bibliography of recent publications on socialist
rural development prepared for the Ford Foundation consists
principally of articles on the planning and management of

rural construction, rural credit, rural medical services, rural libraries, extension services and agricultural development. All the citations were taken from the books and periodicals of the Soviet Bloc countries, not from Western scholars. The majority of the citations were taken from 1969-1973 Soviet Bloc publications, although a few items from earlier years are also included."

Chinese Communist press publications are not included. Items that have been translated are so indicated. Citations also provide location and call numbers for the Library of Congress, the National Agricultural Library and/or the National Library of Medicine.

Entries are annotated and arranged by country and then by author. There are no indexes.

130.  Philippine Council for Agriculture and Resources Research. Bibliography of Research Studies in Agricultural Economics and Applied Rural Sociology, 1969-1975. Los Baños, Laguna, Philippines:  Socio-Economic Research Division, PCARR, 1976. Unavailable for annotation.

131.  Pray, Carl E., and Chitrita B. Abdullah. A Select Bibliography on Agricultural Economics and Rural Development with Special Reference to Bangladesh. Supplement II. BARC Agricultural Economics and Rural Social Science Papers, no. 8. Dacca:  Bangladesh Agricultural Research Council, 1980. x + 61p.

The original volume and Supplement I were compiled by Edward Clay and Mavis Clay. This supplement covers the period from the beginning of 1978 to February 1980. The classification scheme remains essentially the same as in Supplement I. The work concludes with an author index to this supplement only.

132.  Preliminary Listing of Research Studies on Philippine Agrarian Reform from 1972 to the Present. [College, Laguna, Philippines:  Agrarian Reform Institute, 1976.]  4 leaves.

This is a brief bibliography of research primarily done through Philippine institutes, universities, and government departments. Arrangement is alphabetical by author within a section on completed research and a section on ongoing research. It is available at the Land Tenure Center Library, University of Wisconsin, Madison.

133. Reyes-Garcia, H. Integrated Rural Development:
     Country Profile; Inventory of Programmes, Institu-
     tions and Bibliography--Philippines. CIRDAP Study
     Series, no. 14. Quezon City, Philippines: National
     Council on Integrated Rural Development, 1982.
     Unavailable for annotation.

134. Rogers, David L.; Larry Whiting; and Judy A. Ander-
     son. An Annotated Bibliography of Rural Develop-
     ment Research in the North Central Region. Ames:
     North Central Regional Center for Rural Develop-
     ment, Iowa State University, 1975. 229p. ED 108
     839.
     The primary purpose of this bibliography is to list
applied research done by scientists at Agricultural Experiment Stations in the twelve states of the North Central Region: Illinois, Indiana, Iowa, Kansas, Michigan, Minnesota,
Missouri, Nebraska, North Dakota, Ohio, South Dakota, and
Wisconsin. The research reported was conducted between
1967 and 1974. The bibliography is organized into eight
chapters: "Population," "Economic Development Opportunities," "Economic Services," "Social Services," "Environment
and Natural Resources," "Individual and Family Decision
Making," "Group and Community Decision making," and
"General Rural Development Theory." There are no indexes.

135. Rogers, David L., and Ed Shinn. Rural Development
     Case Studies: Bibliography. Fort Collins: Dept.
     of Sociology, Colorado State University, 1983.
     Each entry in this extensive bibliography provides
bibliographic data as well as a brief description of the work.
Primary arrangement is by geographical region. Each entry
is extensively coded to reflect geographical region and level,
subject matter, primary change agent, and teaching key
(whether or not the case is designed for classroom use).
There are no indexes.

136. "Rural Development and Rural Education: Bibliogra-
     phy," Educafrica 1, no. 1 (1974):71-75.
     After a section on bibliographies and one devoted to
citations to general sources, the remainder of the bibliography is devoted to rural development and rural education in
Africa. Most citations are from works published in the
1960's or 1970's and include both English and French language publications. UN publications are heavily emphasized.

137.  Rural Transformation:  A Select Annotated Bibliography
      of Special Programmes.  Rajendranagar, Hyderabad,
      India:  National Institute of Rural Development,
      1984.  269p.
      Unavailable for annotation.

138.  Schmidt, P.  Experimental Selected Bibliography on
      Integrated Rural Development.  Pedagogy and
      Methodology for Development, Series III, no. 1.
      Geneva, Switzerland:  Pan African Institute for
      Development, 1978.  49p.
      This selected bibliography lists works in English,
French, and Spanish, most of which were published between
1970 and 1977.  Books, journal articles, UN documents, and
published and unpublished research papers are the focus of
the bibliography which is organized into subject chapters
within which arrangement is alphabetical by author.  Items
of special importance are starred.  There is an author index
and appendices listing periodicals cited and Institutes and
Documentation Centres consulted in the preparation of the
bibliography.

139.  Selnick, Irwin S.  Agrarian Radicalism and the Green
      Revolution in India 1965-1977:  A Bibliographic Es-
      say and Annotated Bibliography.  [New York:  The
      Author?], 1978.  56p.
      The selected and annotated bibliography section of
this work lists monographs and journal articles by author
within five main subject categories:  "General Works," "Who
Can Participate in the Green Revolution," "The Commerciali-
zation of Agriculture," "Sharing the Rewards of the Green
Revolution," and "The Green Revolution and Agrarian Radicalism."  There is an author index.

140.  Sharma, Prakash C.  Agricultural Planning and Co-
      operatives in India:  A Selected Research Bibliog-
      raphy.  Part I (1944-1963), Part II (1964-1972).
      Exchange Bibliography, no. 667.  Monticello, IL:
      Council of Planning Librarians, 1974.  23p.
      Nearly 150 references are arranged by author within
the two sections of this bibliography.  Monographs, journal
articles, and Indian government publications are emphasized.

141.  Sharma, Prakash C.  Planning for Agricultural and
      Rural Development in Pakistan (1950-1970):  A
      Selected Research Bibliography.  Exchange

Bibliography, no. 727. Monticello, IL: Council of
Planning Librarians, 1975. 12p.
This selected bibliography lists approximately 150
items, most of which were published between 1950 and 1970.
The first part of the bibliography lists books and monographs; the second, articles and periodicals. Publications
of the Pakistan government are included in both sections.
Arrangement is by author within each section. There are
no indexes.

142. Sharma, Prakash C. Rural and Economic Development
     Planning in Bangladesh (formerly East Pakistan):
     A Selected Research Bibliography. Exchange Bib-
     liography, no. 723. Monticello, IL: Council of
     Planning Librarians, 1975. 18p.
This bibliography is divided into sections: Part I
contains material published primarily between 1950 and 1965;
Part II, materials published chiefly between 1966 and 1972.
Within each of these two parts are two sections, one for books
and monographs, the other for articles and periodicals. The
bibliography also includes dissertations, unpublished reports,
conference papers, and many publications of the Pakistan
Academy for Rural Development. Arrangement within sections is by author.

143. Singh, Mohinder, and R.N. Sharma. Rural Develop-
     ment: A Select Bibliography. New Delhi: Uppal
     Publishing House, 1978. 336p.
"The objective of this bibliography is to draw the
attention of practitioners and researchers in the field to the
vast literature covering various aspects of the subject, particularly, rural development policies, planning, programmes,
rural institutions, and village and area studies. Over 3,600
references contained in this bibliography cover macro and
micro literature including books, public documents, research
reports, dissertations, and articles."
        The bibliography is not limited by date and is or-
ganized alphabetically by author within subject chapters and
sub-chapters--e.g., "Rural Development in General," "Policy,
Planning and Programmes," and "Rural Administration."
While some general works are included, the strong emphasis
in the bibliography is on rural development in India. The
bibliography concludes with an author index.

144. Slattery, Alice. Agricultural and Rural Development in

Kenya (A Select Annotated Bibliography, 1960-
1981). [Nairobi?]: U.S. Agency for International
Development, 1982. 336 leaves.
   This bibliography of nearly 900 items, most of
which are annotated, was compiled by searching major
sources such as World Agricultural Economics and Rural
Sociology Abstracts, Kenya Agricultural Abstracts, Farming Systems in Africa: A Working Bibliography, 1930-1978,
etc. The bibliography is arranged by author into 27 subject chapters. Many of these subjects relate to economic or
agricultural topics such as soils, crop production, credit,
etc. A smaller number of chapters deals with social issues
--e.g., rural administration, organization, etc. There are
no indexes.

145. Small Farmer Development. Occasional Bibliography,
     no. 6. Nepal: Agricultural Projects Services Cen-
     ter, Agricultural Documentation Centre, 1980. ii +
     27p.
     Unavailable for annotation.

146. Snell, John P. Tanzania, An Annotated Bibliography
     on Population Within the Context of Rural Develop-
     ment. [Rome: Food and Agriculture Organization,
     1980?] 76 + 23 leaves.
     This bibliography includes a variety of publications
on Tanzanian rural population. All entries were published
outside of Tanzania between 1975 and 1980. The bibliography
is organized into several subject chapters and sub-chapters,
within which entries are arranged by year of publication and
then by author. Entries also include call numbers for items
owned by FAO. Three annexes provide a list of sources of
information, an author index, and a secondary subject index.

147. Southern Rural Development Center, and Mitchell
     Memorial Library, Mississippi State University.
     Rural Development Literature: An Annotated Bib-
     liography, 1969-1975. Prepared for the National
     Agricultural Library. Washington, D.C.: Rural
     Development Service, U.S. Dept. of Agriculture,
     1976. ED 156 407.
     Included in this bibliography are books, articles,
government documents and reports, and ERIC documents
that are concerned with rural development in the U.S. A
few local studies were included but the emphasis is on publications dealing with national or regional studies.

Designed for community leaders, rural development committees, researchers, and community resource development personnel, the bibliography includes information on obtaining the documents listed and also provides information on other sources of information. The latter include names and addresses of government agencies as well as sources of printed information--i.e., directories, guides, primary journals and newsletters, indexes, and on-line searches.

The bibliography is organized into seven subject areas: fire and emergency services, health care delivery systems, sanitary services and sewage systems, manpower training and vocational education, public recreational facilities and planning, local government structure and taxation, and rural housing. Within each section entries are arranged by year and then by author. There are no indexes.

148. Special Bibliography: Environmental Basis for Integrated Rural Development. Bangkok: Asian Development Institute Library and Documentation Centre, 1977. 28p.
Unavailable for annotation.

149. Trong, N.T., and N.D. Kiew. Integrated Rural Development: Country Profile; Inventory of Programmes, Institutions and Bibliography--Vietnam. CIRDAP Study Series, no. 16, 1982.
Unavailable for annotation.

150. UNESCO Regional Office for Education in Asia. Documents on Rural Development and Rural Education. Bangkok: UNESCO, 1970. 27p.
Unavailable for annotation.

151. United Nations. Centre for Regional Development. India: An Annotated Bibliography on Rural Regional Development. Country Bibliography Series, no. 2. Nagoya, [Japan]: The Centre, 1978. viii + 106p.
"References contained in this bibliography focus on rural regional development in India during the past fifteen years.... The information sources are primarily Indian, but a few significant documents of foreign imprints have also been included. All documents referred to are in English and include reference works, government publications, scholarly works (monographs), conference proceedings, and periodical articles."

The annotated entries appear in the last section of
the bibliography and are arranged by UNCRD accession number.  Because of this arrangement the preceding four indexes
--KWIC (keyword in context) title index, subject index, author index, and title index--are essential for the use of the
bibliography.

152.  United Nations.  Centre for Regional Development.
      Sri Lanka:  An Annotated Bibliography on Rural
      Regional Development.  Country Bibliography Ser-
      ies, no. 4.  Nagoya, [Japan]:  The Centre, 1981.
      103p.
      This bibliography lists primarily journal articles and
reports of Sri Lankan institutes, agencies, and organizations.
Most citations are to works published in the 1970's.  There
are indexes by author, title, and subject.  The main section
is the Register which provides a bibliographic description and
annotation for each item.

153.  United Nations Economic and Social Commission for Asia
      and the Pacific.  Library.  Rural Development:  A
      Select Bibliography.  Bibliographical Series, no.
      D.4.  New York:  United Nations, 1982.  99p.
      A reproduction of a computer print-out from the
ESCAP Bibliographic System, "the bibliography comprises 315
records of monographs, documents and serial articles received
in the ESCAP Library during late 1981 to early 1982."
      Arrangement is by title under seven subject head-
ings:  "Agriculture," "Application of Science and Technology,"
"Health and Social Services," "Human Resources Development
and Institutions," "Industrial Development," "Physical Infrastructure, Natural Resources and Environment," and "Policies
and Planning."  There is a concluding country index covering Bangladesh, India, Indonesia, Malaysia, Nepal, Pakistan,
Papua New Guinea, the Philippines, the Republic of Korea,
Singapore, Sri Lanka, Thailand, and Southeast Asia.

154.  United Nations Economic and Social Commission for Asia
      and the Pacific.  Library.  Rural Development:  A
      Select Bibliography.  Bibliographical Series, no.
      D.5.  New York:  United Nations, 1983.  v + 50p.
      Similar in format to the 1982 publication of the same
title, "the bibliography comprises 207 records of monographs,
documents and serial articles received in the ESCAP Library
during the second part of 1982."  There are concluding author, title, and area indexes.

155. Vasiliades, Kanella C., and Cecille Shannon. Bibliog-
     raphy for Programming for Agriculture. EDI Semi-
     nar Paper, no. 6. Washington, D.C.: Economic
     Development Institute, International Bank for Re-
     construction and Development, 1973. 43p.
     The 482 items in this bibliography are listed alpha-
betically by author, without subject division or indexes.
Both published and unpublished works, primarily from the
1960's and 1970's, are included. There is no restriction by
geographical region.

156. Voth, Donald E., and William S. Bonner. Citizen Par-
     ticipation in Rural Development: A Bibliography.
     SRDC Bibliography Series, no. 6. Mississippi State:
     Southern Rural Development Center, 1977. 493p.
     ED 156 408.
     There are 2,310 citations listed in this bibliography;
about one-fourth of them are annotated. "Materials come
from computerized information services, published bibliographies, and books or articles. Citizen participation is here
defined as individual or group activities of ordinary citizens
in their efforts to influence public policy, decision making,
and implementation. Primary emphasis is on administrative,
sponsored, and voluntary participation, with little attention
to political participation.... Though a few entries from the
30's appear, most are from the 60's and 70's; there is
an addendum of 50 items found after December 1976. Citations are arranged alphabetically by author and identified by
a code number through which entries are classified into 31
functional areas at the end of the bibliography."

157. Voth, Donald E., and William S. Bonner. Citizen Par-
     ticipation in Rural Development: A Bibliography.
     SRDC Bibliography Series, no. 6. Supplement.
     Mississippi State: Southern Rural Development
     Center, 1978. 37p. ED 156 409.
     This bibliography is fully annotated and arranged
by author under subject headings. Its purpose is to distill
the larger work of the same title for those persons for whom
the original, extensive work was more frustrating than useful.

158. Watson, Charlotte B. Bibliography for SEADAG Semi-
     nar on Land Reform in the Philippines. [Pines
     Hotel, Baguio, Philippines], April 24-26, 1975.
     3 leaves + 6 leaves.
     Books, journal articles, government documents, and

published and unpublished research papers (including dissertations and theses) are listed without restriction by date.
Arrangement is by author within subject sections, such as
"Agrarian Economy," "Land Reform," "Land Tenure," "Peasant Politics and Unrest," etc. The last six pages are devoted to "New and General Works (since 1972)." The bibliography is available at the Land Tenure Center Library at
the University of Wisconsin-Madison.

159. Watts, Ann DeWitt.  General Annotated Bibliography on
     Rural Development and Planning.  Exchange Bibliog-
     raphy, no. 1397.  Monticello, IL:  Council of Plan-
     ning Librarians, 1977.  18p.
     "This bibliography is intended to be an introductory
resource for persons interested in problems of rural planning
and development.  Many small pieces which are often housed
in out of the way agencies and are hard to find have been
written on the topic.  Some of these difficult to find pieces
have been included in this report, but an attempt has been
made to include primarily items which are still in print and
can be easily obtained.  In addition to articles, books and
pamphlets, general resources, agencies, and other bibliographies ... have been included in this bibliography."  Items
selected were all published in the 1970's.
     The main section of the bibliography, "Rural Devel-
opment and Planning," is divided into eight sub-sections:
"Development," "Health," "Housing," "Manpower," "Planning
and General Information," "Recreation," "Waste Disposal,"
and "Water and Sewer."  The last three sections list agencies and organizations, bibliographies, and newspapers and
journals.  Arrangement within sections or sub-sections is by
author or name of agency.  There are no indexes.

160. Wijk-Sijbesma, Christine van.  Participation and Educa-
     tion in Community Water Supply and Sanitation Pro-
     grammes:  A Selected and Annotated Bibliography.
     Bulletin, no. 13.  The Hague, The Netherlands:
     WHO International Reference Centre for Community
     Water Supply, 1979.  238p.
     Lists 145 selected journal articles, books, and dis-
sertations and other unpublished papers by author.  In addition to bibliographic information, each entry provides the
date and country of research, an extensive annotation, and
a list of keywords.  Selection was intended to include citations to "projects in which either the inclusion or the

exclusion of a participation or education component had demonstrable effects on the success of those projects." The bibliography concludes with indexes by author, keyword, and country.

161. Wood, Garland P., and Kenneth Schwedel. Rural Development Administration: An Annotated Bibliography, [1976?]. 86p.
    Resulting from an A.I.D. contract to "develop a framework for analyzing agricultural institutions, especially in the LDC's [less developed countries]," this bibliography lists readings that "vary greatly in depth of perception, from descriptive to highly theoretical, from first drafts to polished manuscripts."
    The bibliography is organized into nine subject chapters: "Methodology and Comparative Studies," "Systematic Institutional Linkage Module," "Intra-Institution Status Role Study," "Institutional Interfaces," "Communication Flows Within Institutions and to Clientele," "Leadership Characteristics of Institutions," "Farmer Clientele Study," "Evaluation," and "Workshop Approaches and Materials." Annotations are extensive. The bibliography concludes with an author index.

162. Zamora, M.C. Bibliography on Green Revolution, 1975-1976. Occasional Paper, no. 6. College, Laguna, Philippines: Agricultural Libraries Association of the Philippines, University of the Philippines at Los Baños, 1977. 14p.
    This partially annotated bibliography lists articles dealing with the socioeconomic effects of the green revolution. All citations are to articles published during 1975-1976. Arrangement is alphabetical by author. There is a concluding subject index.

163. Zewdie Kumilachew. A Selected Bibliography on Rural Development. Addis Ababa: Documents Dept., Addis Ababa University Libraries, 1977. 12 leaves.
    Conference proceedings, reports of institutes, organizations, and universities, and government documents are all included in this brief bibliography. Periodical literature is excluded. Most items have publication dates in the 1960's or 1970's. There is no geographical restriction.

164. Zuvekas, Clarence. An Annotated Bibliography of

Agricultural Development in Bolivia. Bolivia, Working Document, no. 1. [Washington, D.C.]: Rural
Development Bureau for Latin America, [U.S.]
Agency for International Development, 1977. iv +
162 p.
    Listing works representing a variety of languages,
but primarily Spanish and English, this bibliography emphasizes "credit, marketing, nutrition, technology, income distribution, and employment." With few exceptions only works
published since 1952 are included.
    The bibliography is arranged in one list by author.
There are no indexes, but abbreviations for one or more of
the subject areas emphasized appear next to each entry.

165. Zuvekas, Clarence. An Annotated Bibliography of
      Agricultural Development in Haiti. Working Docu-
      ment Series, General Working Document, no. 1.
      [Washington]: Rural Development Division, Bureau
      for Latin America, [U.S.] Agency for International
      Development, 1977. iv + 106p.
    Both French and English language publications are
included in this bibliography. "The specific areas covered
are credit, marketing, nutrition, technology, income distribution, and employment." With a few exceptions, only works
published since 1950 are included.
    Arrangement is alphabetical by author. There are
no indexes, but abbreviations for one or more of the five
subject areas emphasized appear next to each entry.

# EDUCATION

166. Altus, David M. Migrant Education, A Selected Bibliography. Supplement, no. 2. Las Cruces: Educational Resources Information Center, Clearinghouse on Rural Education and Small Schools, New Mexico State University, 1971. 140p. ED 055 706.
"Ninety documents and 44 journal articles published between 1964 and 1970 are cited in this bibliography on migrant education. Part I contains citations and abstracts which have appeared in 'Research in Education' from June 1970 through March 1971. Part II includes citations of journal articles from 'Current Index to Journals in Education' from the first issue in January 1969 through the July 1971 issue. The citations include a wide variety of resource materials (research and program reports, guides, books, etc.) which examine educational needs of migrant families and educational programs for migrant youth and adults." There is a subject index.

167. Bochet, J.C. "Education for Rural Development," Educational Documentation and Information 54, no. 216 (1980):1-97.
Several languages are represented in this annotated bibliography of works published between 1975 and 1979. The bibliography is intended to update the one appearing in Educational Documentation and Information no. 183 (1972) as well as one appearing in the 1974 UNESCO publication Education in a Rural Environment.
The bibliography is divided into the following subject headings: "General," "Development Planning," "Adult Education," "Educational Programmes and Content," "Methods: Communication, Technology, Teaching," "Schools and Colleges," "Higher Education," and "Non-formal Education." Within further sub-divisions arrangement is alphabetical by author. There is an author and an editor index.

168. Commonwealth Bureau of Agricultural Economics. Ex-
    tension and Advisory Services--Africa, 1973-1980.
    Annotated Bibliography, no. R46. Commonwealth
    Agricultural Bureaux, 1981. 62p.
    Unavailable for annotation. Secondary sources indi-
    cate that this bibliography covers CAB indexes for the period
    1973-1980 and lists 198 citations.

169. Conley, Howard K. An Annotated Bibliography on Dis-
    sertations on American Indian, Mexican American,
    Migrant and Rural Education. Las Cruces: Educa-
    tional Resources Information Center, Clearinghouse
    on Rural Education and Small Schools, New Mexico
    State University, 1973. 50p. ED 080 251.
    "An annotated bibliography covering American Indi-
    an, Mexican American, migrant and rural education, this doc-
    ument includes doctoral dissertations written between 1964-
    1972. There are 62 entries for American Indians, 26 for
    Mexican Americans, 7 for migrants and 8 for rural and small
    schools. A subject index ends the document."

170. Deaton, Brady J., and Kevin T. McNamara. Education
    in a Changing Rural Environment: The Impact of
    Population and Economic Change on the Demand for
    and Costs of Public Education in Rural America: A
    Synthesis of Research Findings and an Identification
    of Important Policy Issues. SRDC Synthesis-
    Bibliography Series, no. 18. Mississippi State:
    Southern Rural Development Center, 1984. 89p.
    ED 241 210.
    The bibliography portion of this combined synthesis/
    bibliography appears on pages 41 to 78. It is annotated and
    "describes 121 research reports published between 1960 and
    1983." Citations are restricted to works concerning the U.S.
    There are no indexes.

171. De Vries, James. Selected Bibliography on Agricultural
    Extension in Tanzania. Technical Paper, no. 3.
    Morogoro, Tanzania: Dept. of Rural Economy,
    Faculty of Agriculture, Forestry and Veterinary
    Science, University of Dar es Salaam, 1978. iii +
    44p.
    "This publication lists titles that contain material on
    agricultural extension and related topics, with particular em-
    phasis on Tanzania and nearby countries. It includes only

post-independence publications and major unpublished material.  References are listed under the following topics with
cross-references as required:  General, philosophy, organization, administration, adoption and diffusion of innovations,
communication, teaching and learning, extension methods,
planning, evaluation, staff training, and farmer training."

172.  Dyk, D.V.  Audio-Visual Techniques for Rural Devel-
      opment:  A Working Bibliography.  East Lansing:
      African Rural Economy Program, Dept. of Agricul-
      tural Economics, Michigan State University, 1980.
      17p.
      Unavailable for annotation.

173.  "Education for Rural Life," Educational Documentation
      and Information, Bulletin of the International Bureau
      of Education 46, no. 183 (1972):29-142.
      The emphasis in this bibliography is on material
published between 1965 and 1970 concerning rural education
in developing countries.  Several languages are represented
in the bibliography.  The principal source of material selected
was the IBE library.  A wide range of publications, excluding periodical articles, is included.
      The bibliography is arranged by author within six
chapters:  "Bibliographies on rural education," "Factors in
rural background," "Policies, planning and economics of rural
education," "Organizational and curricular aspects," "Teach-
ers--recruitment, training, retraining," and "Needs of different rural groups."  There is a concluding author index,
countries index, and subject index.

174.  Egner, Joan Roos, and Deborah Rassol Friedman.
      Policy Making in Rural Education Institutions:  An
      Annotated Bibliography.  Ithaca:  Dept. of Educa-
      tion, New York State College of Agriculture and
      Life Sciences, Cornell University, 1977.  82p.
      This bibliography is focused on issues of education-
al governance in rural K-12 school districts and community
colleges.  Included are books, periodical articles, government documents, dissertations, and ERIC documents.  Most
were written in the 1970's.  The bibliography is organized
into eleven subject chapters within which arrangement is
alphabetical by author.  There are no indexes.

175.  Fuller, Jack, et al.  "A Selected Bibliography on Rural

Life and Education," Community College Frontiers 7,
no. 2 (Winter 1979):54-55.
The emphasis in this brief bibliography is books
and journal articles concerning rural U.S. colleges. All citations are to works published in the 1970's.

176.  Heathman, James E., and Alyce J. Nafzinger. Migrant
      Education, A Selected Bibliography. Supplement
      No. 1. Las Cruces: Educational Resources Infor-
      mation Center, Clearinghouse on Rural Education
      and Small Schools, New Mexico State University,
      1970. 44p. ED 040 002.
The original bibliography on migrant education was
published in 1969. This supplement contains approximately
75 citations and abstracts that appeared in Resources in Education from February 1969 through June 1970. The education of migrant children and adults is covered. There is a
concluding subject index.

177.  Hughes, Jane Barron. Rural Library Service. Occa-
      sional Bibliography, no. 3. Clarion, PA: Center
      for the Study of Rural Librarianship, School of Li-
      brary Science, Clarion State College, 1979. 25p.
      ED 183 339.
"... This document lists over 800 entries dealing
with the specific concerns of rural, county, and small community libraries. Listed alphabetically by author under
subject headings, the entries cover the period from 1930 to
1975 and are drawn from a variety of sources including educational journals, regional and national library journals,
foreign and international library journals, books, conference proceedings, government publications, and theses and
dissertations. The 16 subject headings relate to the role of
the rural public library, characteristics of rural communities
and populations, and the role of libraries with respect to
adult education. Specific topics include library extension
and outreach, finance, professional training for rural librarians, rural reading interests, rural school libraries, rural
communications, and rural development."

178.  International Institute for Adult Literacy Methods,
      Library. Rural Education: A Select Bibliography.
      ILEP Seminar Paper, no. 22. Paris: International
      Institute for Educational Planning, United Nations
      Educational, Scientific, and Cultural Organization,
      1975. 12p. ED 135 534.

"Including 120 citations, this selected bibliography
on rural education covers the period between 1967 and 1975
and presents entries representative of the developing nations. Major subject areas are: women, rural youth, integrated rural development, adult education, nonformal education, employment, educational planning and development,
mass communication, evaluation and lifelong education."
Arrangement is in one alphabetical list by author. There
are no indexes.

179.  Kniefel, David R., and Tanya S. Kniefel. Annotated
       Bibliography and Descriptive Summary of Disserta-
       tions and Theses on Rurality and Small Schools.
       Las Cruces: Educational Resources Information
       Center, Clearinghouse on Rural Education and
       Small Schools, New Mexico State University, 1970.
       51p. ED 039 962.
       "The 76 citations listed and annotated in this bib-
liography were selected from Volumes 25 through 29 (1965-
1969) of 'Dissertations Abstracts.' The dissertations and
theses, bearing completion dates from 1963 through 1968,
were selected from 3 major subject areas: rural sociology,
rural education, and small schools. The major intent of the
bibliography is to provide a comprehensive source of research efforts on rurality and small schools. The presentation is intended for sociologists, researchers, and practitioners. The majority of entries in the bibliography may be
categorized under the following ERIC descriptors: econom-
ically disadvantaged, occupational aspiration, rural urban
differences, rural youth, and small schools. A subject index of ERIC descriptors is appended."

180.  Leathers, Roxanna M., and 'Matsaba J. Leballo.
       Extension in Lesotho: Bibliography of Materials
       Available in Maseru. LASA Special Bibliography,
       no. 1. [Fort Collins]: Lesotho Agricultural Sec-
       tor Analysis Project, Dept. of Economics, Colorado
       State University, 1979. 10 leaves.
       Items listed in this bibliography are available in one
of six libraries. Location information is provided for each
item.
       Arrangement is alphabetical by author within three
sections: "Extension and Training in Lesotho," "General
Reference on Extension Available Locally," and "Recent Extension Materials Issued by the Agricultural Information
Service."

181.  Lewis, Nancy H.  Training, Management and Evaluation
       of Extension Work, 1970-1978.  Quick Bibliography
       Series, no. 78-11.  Beltsville, MD:  National Agri-
       cultural Library, 1978.
          This bibliography lists 278 citations to relevant
English language publications from the Agricola data base.
The format is a reproduction of the computer print-out.
There are no indexes.

182.  Magisos, Joel H., and Anne E. Stakelon.  Special
       Needs Populations:  Annotated Bibliographies on
       Bilingual, Correctional, Migrant, and Handicapped
       Populations with Unique Vocational Education Needs.
       Bibliography Series, no. 33.  Columbus:  The Cen-
       ter for Vocational Education, Ohio State University,
       1975.  142p.  ED 133 607.
          Pages 59 to 72 of this bibliography list selected
items pertaining to migrant education and social/economic
conditions.  Items were taken from Resources in Education,
Current Index to Journals in Education, and Abstracts of
Instructional and Research Materials in Vocational Technical
Education.

183.  Massey, Sara.  Rural Education:  An Annotated Bibli-
       ography.  Machias:  University of Maine, 1982.
       31p.  ED 218 030.
          Books, journal articles, conference proceedings,
newsletters, etc. are included in this bibliography which is
arranged into six sections.  "Section I includes those materials on rural education which provide an overview or comprehensive perspective, definitions, or demographics.  Sections II-IV include materials which address major rural education issues:  school organization, financing, and legislation; staff recruitment and maintenance; instruction and
services.  Section V provides a listing of organizations,
journals, and films which deal with rural topics.  Section VI
lists other resources which relate to rural topics or may be
of interest to those studying rural education."

184.  McClymont, D.S.  A Selected Bibliography of Agricul-
       tural Extension and Agricultural Education Publica-
       tions in Zimbabwe.  Salisbury:  Institute of Adult
       Education, University of Zimbabwe, 1981.  45p.
       Unavailable for annotation.

185.  Migrant Education, A Selected Bibliography (with ERIC
      abstracts). Supplement No. 3. Las Cruces: Edu-
      cational Resources Information Center, Clearinghouse
      on Rural Education and Small Schools, New Mexico
      State University, 1973. 167p. ED 075 162.
   This supplement includes citations from Resources
in Education from April 1971 through September 1972 and
from Current Index to Journals in Education from December
1970 through September 1972. There is a subject index.

186.  Migrant Education, A Selected Bibliography (with ERIC
      abstracts). Supplement No. 4. Las Cruces: Edu-
      cational Resources Information Center, Clearinghouse
      on Rural Education and Small Schools, New Mexico
      State University, 1974. 140p. ED 087 599.
   This supplement contains citations and abstracts
from Resources in Education and Current Index to Journals
in Education from October 1972 through December 1973.
"Entries include a wide variety of resource materials such as
research and program reports, teacher guides, and doctoral
dissertations. Some major areas of emphasis are bilingual
education and Elementary and Secondary Education Act Programs. Subject indexes and ordering information are appended."

187.  Migrant Education, A Selected Bibliography (with ERIC
      abstracts). Supplement No. 5. Las Cruces: Edu-
      cational Resources Information Center, Clearinghouse
      on Rural Education and Small Schools, New Mexico
      State University, 1975. ED 101 909. 123p.
   "Part 1 contains citations and abstracts which appeared in 'Resources in Education' (RIE) from January 1974
through December 1974. Part 2 includes citations of journal
articles which appeared in 'Current Index to Journals in Education' (CIJE) from January 1974 through December 1974.
The citations cover such topics as agricultural laborers,
Mexican Americans, migrant child education, program evalua-
tions, migrant workers, and migrants. A combined RIE and
CIJE subject index is provided...."

188.  Migrant Education, A Selected Bibliography (with ERIC
      abstracts). Supplement No. 6. Las Cruces: Edu-
      cational Resources Information Center, Clearinghouse
      on Rural Education and Small Schools, New Mexico
      State University, 1976. 131p. ED 118 292.

"Part 1 contains 82 citations and abstracts which appeared in 'Resources in Education' (RIE) from January 1975 through December 1975. Part 2 includes 21 citations of journal articles which appeared in 'Current Index to Journals in Education' (CIJE) from January 1975 through December 1975. The citations cover such topics as agricultural laborers, educational programs, federal programs and legislation, human services, Mexican Americans, migrant child education, migrant workers, outreach programs, rural education and summer programs." There is a combined RIE and CIJE index.

189. Migrant Education, A Selected Bibliography (with ERIC abstracts). Supplement No. 7. Las Cruces: Educational Resources Information Center, Clearinghouse on Rural Education and Small Schools, New Mexico State University, 1977. 213p. ED 139 549.
This supplemental bibliography lists 175 citations and abstracts from Resources in Education from January through December 1976 and 14 citations and abstracts from Current Index to Journals in Education for the same period. Subjects covered include social and economic aspects of migrants' lives as well as educational programs designed for migrant adults and children. There is a subject index.

190. Migrant Education, A Bibliography of ERIC Abstracts. Supplement No. 8. Las Cruces: Educational Resources Information Center, Clearinghouse on Rural Education and Small Schools, New Mexico State University, 1978. 172p. ED 151 109.
This supplement lists 120 citations and abstracts from Resources in Education from January through October 1977 and 40 citations and abstracts from Current Index to Journals in Education for the same period. A wide variety of materials is included covering economic and social as well as educational issues in migrants' lives. There is a subject index.

191. Norell, Irene P. "Rural Libraries: A Selective Annotated Bibliography," Rural Libraries 2, no. 1 (Winter 1982):67-105.
This bibliography results from a computer search of the ERIC data base through September 1, 1981. The subject is user needs and library services in rural areas and communities with a population of fewer than 10,000.

192. Palmer, Barbara C.  Migrant Education:  An Annotated
     Bibliography.  Newark, DE:  International Reading
     Assoc., 1982.  66p.  ED 214 724.
     "Materials selected for inclusion in the annotated
bibliography of 139 publications from 1970 to 1980 give a
general understanding of the lives of migrant children, their
educational needs and problems, and various attempts to
meet those needs.  The bibliography ... includes books, dissertations, articles, conference papers and government documents divided into five major categories:  General Information, Characteristics of Migrant Children, Education of Migrant Children, Education Programs for Migrant Children,
and Bibliographies."

193. Rural Education.  Literacy Bibliographies, no. 9.
     Tehran, Iran:  International Institute for Adult
     Literacy Methods, 1977.  44p.
     This bibliography includes a wide range of publi-
cations in English, French, or Spanish, most of which were
published in the 1970's.  The focus of the bibliography is
adult, nontraditional education as it relates to rural development.  The bibliography is organized into one alphabetical
list by author.  There are no indexes.

194. Siegrist, Edith B.  South Dakota Country School Bib-
     liography:  An Annotated List of References Relat-
     ing to Country Schools in the Collection of I.D.
     Weeks Library, The University of South Dakota.
     Silt, CO:  Country Legacy Project, Mountain Plains
     Library Assoc., 1981.  25p.  ED 211 270.
     "Materials from the I.D. Weeks Library of the Uni-
versity of South Dakota relating to country schools and the
history of rural education in South Dakota and written between 1874 and 1976, are listed in this annotated bibliography."

195. Small Schools, A Selected Bibliography (with ERIC ab-
     stracts).  Las Cruces:  Educational Resources In-
     formation Center, Clearinghouse on Rural Education
     and Small Schools, New Mexico State University,
     1974.  43p.  ED 097 185.
     This bibliography contains citations and abstracts
from Resources in Education and Current Index to Journals
in Education from the period April 1973 through June 1974.
Previously, information on small schools was included in the

ERIC bibliography series on rural education. This new bibliography series is not restricted to small schools in rural areas. "The scope of small school coverage is: economic, cultural, social or other factors related to educational programs of small schools (public, private or parochial) located in urban or rural settings." There is a subject index.

196. Small Schools, A Selected Bibliography (with ERIC abstracts). Supplement No. 1. Las Cruces: Educational Resources Information Center, Clearinghouse on Rural Education and Small Schools, New Mexico State University, 1975. 64p. ED 107 416.
    This bibliography supplements earlier bibliographies in the series on rural education and small schools. Included are citations from Resources in Education and Current Index to Journals in Education for the period July 1974 through March 1975. "A wide variety of material (program descriptions, annual reports, technical reports, etc.) is covered, particularly in the areas of higher education, educational administration, and educational finance." There is a subject index.

197. Small Schools, A Selected Bibliography (with ERIC abstracts). Supplement No. 2. Las Cruces: Educational Resources Information Center, Clearinghouse on Rural Education and Small Schools, New Mexico State University, 1976. 64p. ED 125 807.
    Citations and abstracts from Resources in Education and Current Index to Journals in Education from April 1975 through March 1976 are listed in this bibliography. "A wide variety of material (program descriptions, technical reports, bibliographies, etc.) is covered, particularly in the areas of elementary/secondary education, rural schools, and educational problems." There is a subject index.

198. Small Schools, A Selected Bibliography (with ERIC abstracts). Supplement No. 3. Las Cruces: Educational Resources Information Center, Clearinghouse on Rural Education and Small Schools, New Mexico State University, 1977. 59p. ED 141 059.
    This supplemental bibliography covers citations and abstracts from Resources in Education and Current Index to Journals in Education from April 1976 through May 1977. A wide range of type of material and subjects related to small schools is included. There is a subject index.

199. Styler, W.E. A Bibliographical Guide to Adult Educa-
      tion in Rural Areas 1918-1972. Hull, U.K.: Dept.
      of Adult Education, University of Hull, 1973. 50p.
      ED 074 340.
      Books, pamphlets, periodical articles, and govern-
ment documents are included in this extensive bibliographical
guide to works related to education for adults in rural areas
of the United Kingdom. Coverage is broad, excluding only
publications dealing solely with agricultural education. The
guide is organized into subject chapters and concludes with
an index of authors.

200. Tonigan, Richard F. Small Schools Bibliography.
      Albuquerque: New Mexico Research and Study
      Council and Bureau of Educational Planning and
      Development, University of New Mexico, 1980.  40p.
      ED 194 283.
      "The more than 220 books, monographs, and arti-
cles listed in Sections I and II of this bibliography pertain
to small schools and small school districts (generally, districts enrolling under 2,500 students) and the 54 school-
community analysis publications listed in Section III pertain
to any size school-community situation.... Publication dates
of the materials range from 1916 through 1980, with the majority occurring in the 1970's."

201. Watts, E.R. "Agricultural Extension in Sub-Saharan
      Africa: A Bibliography," Rural Africana 16 (Fall
      1971):24-35.
      "This selected bibliography consists of books, arti-
cles from periodicals, and conference papers available from
established sources. Government documents, FAO reports,
and duplicated material have normally been omitted unless
there was a reasonable certainty of their availability. An
attempt has been made to gather material from all countries
south of the Sahara. However, coverage is broader for the
English-speaking countries, particularly for East Africa.
The main bibliographic source has been Agricultural Extension in the Developing Countries by C.A. de Vries (published by the International Institute for Land Reclamation
and Improvement, Wageningen, The Netherlands, 1968)."
      The bibliography is annotated and arranged alpha-
betically by author under subject headings.

202. Webb, Maxine W. Feedback in Media Production in

Botswana: An Annotated Bibliography. Gaborone,
Botswana: Documentation Unit, National Institute of
Development and Cultural Research, University College of Botswana, University of Botswana and Swaziland, 1981. v + 26p.
    Most of the items in this bibliography are publica-
tions from within Botswana. Not all but many of them concern the use of media to convey agricultural information.
All were published in the 1970's or 1980. Arrangement is
alphabetical by author. There is a subject index.

203. Wheelock, Gerald, and Pushpa B. Sapra. Educational
     Needs Projection and Rural Development: A Bibli-
     ography. SRDC Bibliography Series, no. 7. Mis-
     sissippi State: Southern Rural Development Center,
     1978. vi + 161p.
    Items included in this bibliography were selected
from Dissertations Abstracts International and from the ERIC
Resources in Education file. The bibliography is organized
into three sections: "Community Involvement and Rural Educational Planning: Selected References from ERIC/RIE,"
"Methodologies for Determining Educational Needs: From
Dissertations Abstracts International," and "Dissertations of
Public School Topics in the South."
    Within each of these chapters, entries are first ar-
ranged in a classified order and then in numerical order,
where more complete bibliographical information is provided.
Indexes by author are provided in the first two chapters
and by author within state in the third section.

# GENERAL

204. Alberta Municipal Affairs. Special Projects and Policy
Research. Small Towns and Rural Communities in
Alberta: A Selected Bibliography, 1975. 6 leaves
+ 3 leaves.
Most of the items listed in this bibliography are
master's theses or reports of local or provincial governments
or commissions. Economic and political documents are included as well as ones related to rural sociology. The bibliography concludes with appendices of General Plans for
Alberta communities as well as reports from the Alberta
Housing Corporation.

205. Altus, David M. Rural Education and Small Schools:
A Selected Bibliography. Supplement No. 1. Las
Cruces: Educational Resources Information Center,
Clearinghouse on Rural Education and Small Schools,
New Mexico State University, 1971. 495p. ED 055
695.
"Some 352 documents and 166 journal articles published between 1955 and 1970 are cited in this bibliography
on rural education and small schools. Part I contains citations and abstracts which have appeared in 'Research in Education' from September 1969 through July 1971. Part II
includes journal articles from 'Current Index to Journals in
Education' from the first issue in January 1969 through the
July 1971 issue. The citations include a wide variety of resource materials (research and program reports, guides,
books, etc.) which examine educational needs, opportunities,
and programs in rural and small schools." There is a subject index.

206. Asian Mass Communication Research and Information
Centre. Communication and Change in Rural Asia:

A Select Bibliography. Communication Bibliogra-
phies, no. 1. Singapore: The Centre, 1973. 50
leaves.
Compiled as a background paper for the Asian Mass
Communication Research and Information Centre's Regional
Conference on Communication and Change in Rural Asia
(Bangalore, August 28-September 3, 1973), this bibliography
lists relevant holdings, excluding periodical articles, in the
Centre's collection. There is an emphasis on unpublished
papers.
The geographical coverage includes all of rural Asia
from Afghanistan to Korea and Indonesia. The bibliography
is arranged by author within nine subject chapters: "The
Communication and Development Process," "Media and Chan-
nels," "Methods and Techniques," "Diffusion of Innovations,"
"Factors Related to Development," "Research and Methodology,"
"Teaching and Training." "Other Subjects," and "Bibliographies." There are no indexes.

207.  Bertrand, Alvin L.  Seventy Years of Rural Sociology
      in the United States:  Abstracts of Articles and
      Bulletin Bibliography.  NY:  Essay Press, 1972.
      428p.
The bulk of this extensive bibliography consists of
abstracts of articles relating to rural sociology. Entries
were selected from U.S. scholarly sociological journals. Each
journal was indexed from the date of its inception, the old-
est being American Journal of Sociology, begun in 1895.
This section is organized into nine subject chapters with
sub-headings within each. Within each sub-chapter entries
are arranged alphabetically by author.
Following this section is an unannotated list of monographs, reports, and bulletins arranged in one list by author.
Items on this list were received and listed by Rural Sociology
from 1936 to 1970. Although unannotated, entries are preceded by a code indicating entry number in the bibliography,
publication year, subject classification, and state where it
was published.
The bibliography concludes with subject, author,
and periodical indexes. The periodical index lists the abstract numbers of the articles taken from each title.

208.  Blaxter, L.  Irish Rural Society:  A Selected Bibliog-
      raphy, 1920-1972.  Belfast, U.K.:  Social Anthro-
      pology Dept., Queen's University, 1972. 45p.
      Unavailable for annotation.

209. Bohren, Lenora. Part-Time and Small Farming: An
   Annotated Bibliography. Washington, D.C.: Economics and Statistics Service, U.S. Dept. of Agriculture, 1980. iii + 84p.
   "While the majority of works cited in this annotated
bibliography pertain to part-time farming in the United
States, the collection includes references to other countries
as well, especially European and South American. The works
are presented alphabetically by author and describe the nature and prevalence of part-time farming, the reasons for it,
its finances, its effect on the farm sector, the enterprises
best suited for part-time farming, etc. A geographic index
at the back of the collection guides the reader to entries
that deal only with a certain country, state, province, or
region."
   The bibliography is not limited by date of publication; there is an emphasis on works published since 1960 in
journals or publications of the U.S. government (especially
Agricultural Experiment Stations).

210. Boles, Donald E., and Gary L. Rupnow. "The Impact
   of Corporate Farming and Rural Land Ownership
   upon Local Communities: A Bibliographic Review,"
   Iowa State Journal of Research 52, no. 4 (May
   1978):473-486.
   After their introduction and overview, the authors
organize their review into sections on "Corporate Farming
and Governmental Action," "Public Policy and Taxation,"
"Land Use Considerations," and "Community Adjustment."
There are 60 items in the list of annotated references at the
conclusion of the review, all of them concerned with corporate farming in the United States.

211. Bollman, Ray D. Selected Annotated Bibliography of
   Research on Part-time Farming in Canada. Public
   Administration Series, no. P-262. Monticello, IL:
   Vance Bibliographies, 1979. 64p.
   Journal articles, books, Canadian federal and pro-
vincial government documents as well as unpublished papers
are listed in chronological order. The annotations are ex-
tensive and the items included date from 1944 to 1977.

212. Broadbent, K.P. The Development of Chinese Agriculture, 1949-1970. Commonwealth Bureau of Agricultural Economics, Annotated Bibliography, no. 3.

Commonwealth Agricultural Bureaux, [1971?] iv +
28p.
   The 225 citations and annotations in this bibliography
were taken from CAB abstracting journals. While many of the
selected items concern economic issues such as marketing,
finance, and credit, others concern rural social issues--
agrarian reform, communes, resettlement, etc. The bibliography concludes with a subject index.

213. Byers, David M., and Bernard Quinn. Readings for
     Town & Country Church Workers: An Annotated
     Bibliography. Washington, D.C.: Glenmary Re-
     search Center, 1974. 121p.
   Intended to provide suggested background reading
in rural sociology for persons undertaking church work in
rural areas, the items in this bibliography were primarily
selected from 10,000 volumes of the Glenmary Research Center Library. The entries have lengthy annotations and include books, government documents, and periodical articles.
Most items were published from the 1960's to early 1970's although some, especially literature, date from as early as the
nineteenth century.
   The bibliography is arranged into eight subject
chapters, e.g., "The Rural Scene," "Community Studies,"
"The Idea of Community," and "Regional Studies." Indexes
are by author and by state, the latter tying together all entries on each state represented.

214. Cohen, John M. A Select Bibliography on Rural
     Ethiopia. Ethiopian Bibliographical Series, no. 4.
     Addis Ababa: Haile Selassie I University Library,
     1971. 82 leaves.
   This bibliography includes books, periodical articles,
government documents, UN documents, theses, dissertations,
and unpublished papers. Most titles listed were published
between 1950 and 1970, although some earlier works are in-
cluded.
   The bibliography is organized into five subject
chapters: "Rural Geography, Resources and Population,"
"Rural Anthropology and Culture," "Rural Sociology and
Community Development," "Rural Political Administration and
Law," and "Rural Agricultural Production and Marketing."
Within chapters the arrangement is alphabetical by author.
The work concludes with a two-page listing of rural Ethiopian
research in progress. There are no indexes.

215. Collette, W. Arden, and Gail Easley. The Role of
     Communication and Attitudes in Small Farm Pro-
     grams: A Bibliography. SRDC Bibliography Se-
     ries, no. 4. Mississippi State: Southern Rural
     Development Center, [1977?] iii + 94p.
   Social science literature from 1955 to the mid-1970's
was selected for this annotated bibliography. Only material
relevant to small farms in the United States is cited. Arrangement is by title. There are author and subject indexes.

216. Commonwealth Bureau of Agricultural Economics.
     Aspects of Agricultural Development in Asia. nos.
     RC 1-4. Compiled by K.P. Broadbent. Common-
     wealth Agricultural Bureaux, 1976-1977. 4 vols.
   The citations and annotations in this four-volume
set were previously published in CAB abstracting journals.
Agricultural as well as social research is included in the
bibliography. Volume I is on West Asia and covers literature published between 1970 and 1975. Volume II is on
South Asia, Volume III, on South East Asia, and Volume IV,
on East Asia. All three of these volumes cover the literature published between 1968 and 1975. Within each volume
there is a general introductory section followed by an arrangement by country and then by author. Volumes range
in length from 35 to 75 pages; some but not all have a subject and/or author index.

217. Commonwealth Bureau of Agricultural Economics. The
     Caribbean, Central America: Agricultural Situation
     and Prospects. Annotated Bibliography, Series D,
     no. 5. Commonwealth Agricultural Bureaux, 1974.
     17p.
   "This bibliography consists of publications already
abstracted in World Agricultural Economics and Rural Sociology Abstracts (WAERSA) from 1965 to 1973.
   "It is arranged in the first place with a general section under the headings: policy, products and sociology;
thereafter geographically. The final arrangement is alphabetically by author." There is a concluding subject index.

218. Commonwealth Bureau of Agricultural Economics. The
     Caribbean, General: Agricultural Situation and
     Prospects. Annotated Bibliography, Series D, no.
     1. Commonwealth Agricultural Bureaux, 1974. 8p.
   This bibliography consists of citations and annotations

that appeared in World Agricultural Economics and Rural
Sociology Abstracts between 1965 and 1973.  The bibliography
is arranged by author within a general section and a products
section.  It concludes with a subject index.

219.  Commonwealth Bureau of Agricultural Economics.  The
      Caribbean, Greater Antilles:  Agricultural Situation
      and Prospects.  Annotated Bibliography, Series D,
      no. 3.  Commonwealth Agricultural Bureaux, 1974.
      15p.
      "This bibliography, the third in a series on the
Caribbean region, consists of publications already abstracted
in World Agricultural Economics and Rural Sociology Abstracts
(WAERSA) from 1965 to 1973.
      "It is divided in the first place according to country.
Within the main country sections the entries are arranged
under the headings:  policy, commodities and social factors,
which are in turn sub-divided by subject where appropriate,
while the final arrangement is alphabetical by author."  There
is a concluding subject index.

220.  Commonwealth Bureau of Agricultural Economics.  The
      Caribbean, Jamaica:  Agricultural Situation and
      Prospects.  Compiled by Ann Thirkell Smith.  An-
      notated Bibliography, Series D, no. 2.  Common-
      wealth Agricultural Bureaux, 1974.  8p.
      "This bibliography consists of publications already
abstracted in World Agricultural Economics and Rural Sociology Abstracts (WAERSA) from 1965 to 1973.
      "It is divided into three main sections:  policy, com-
modities and social factors.  The policy section is in turn
divided into general, land use and marketing; the commodities
are arranged alphabetically after a general section.
      "As well as publications relating specifically to
Jamaica, some more general papers on the Caribbean region
as a whole are included, where these have relevance to the
situation in Jamaica."  The bibliography concludes with a
subject index.

221.  Commonwealth Bureau of Agricultural Economics.  The
      Caribbean, Lesser Antilles:  Agricultural Situation
      and Prospects.  Annotated Bibliography, Series D,
      no. 4.  Commonwealth Agricultural Bureaux, 1974.
      10p.
      "This bibliography consists of publications already

abstracted in World Agricultural Economics and Rural Sociology Abstracts (WAERSA) from 1965 to 1973.
"After a general section on the whole Lesser Antilles, the arrangement is geographical." The bibliography concludes with a subject index.

222. Commonwealth Bureau of Agricultural Economics. Minorities in Rural Areas: An Annotated Bibliography. Annotated Bibliography, no. R38. Commonwealth Agricultural Bureaux, 1976. 8p.

"This bibliography of world literature contains references to material previously abstracted in World Agricultural Economics and Rural Sociology Abstracts (WAERSA) covering the period 1970-1975.

"Abstracts are arranged geographically and include research into migration, political structure, settlement, land rights, education, urbanization and problems of livestock and crop production."

223. Cornell Rural Sociology Bulletin Series. Bibliography of the Department, July 1967-October 1979. Supplement 2 for Bulletin No. 48. Ithaca, NY: Dept. of Rural Sociology, Cornell University, 1979. 59p. ED 197 933.

"The more than 500 items listed in this bibliography of the publications of the Cornell University Department of Rural Sociology for the period July 1, 1967 through October 30, 1979 consist of those published works of present and former staff members which appeared during their affiliations with the Department or were the result of research done while affiliated with the Department, and those publications prepared by graduate students as part of their work for department research and extension programs. Part I lists publications issued by the New York State College of Agriculture and Life Sciences and by the Cornell University Experiment Station: (1) 'Search' (a research monograph series); (2) Cornell University Agricultural Experiment Station bulletin series; (3) New York's Food and Life Sciences bulletin series; (4) Cornell Community and Resource Development bulletin series; (5) Information bulletin series; (6) Cornell International Agriculture bulletin series (7) Cornell International Agriculture mimeograph series; (8) Cornell International Agriculture reprint series; and (9) 4-H publications. Part II lists publications issued by the Department of Rural Sociology: (1) Department of Rural Sociology bulletin series;

(2) Regional Development Studies; (3) special reports; and
(4) Rural Sociology Extension bulletins. Part III lists books,
professional journal articles, and other publications. All
listings are by category and author."

224.  Cosby, Arthur G., and Richard C. Wetherill. Re-
      sources in Evaluation for Rural Development: A
      Bibliography. SRDC Bibliography Series, no. 2.
      Mississippi State: Southern Rural Development
      Center, 1977. iv + 92p. ED 157 649.
      Over 500 citations, primarily to both published and
unpublished works from the 1960's and 1970's, are listed in
this bibliography. "Specific attention is given to evaluation
of rural development programs noneconomic in nature--those
designed to raise overall quality of life, level of living, life
satisfaction, knowledge, and acquisition of leadership and
decision-making skills by rural residents."
      The first section of the bibliography is annotated
and is arranged by author within seven subject divisions:
"Major Sources," "Definitions of Rural Development," "Definitions of Evaluation," "Criteria-Setting," "Strategies of
Evaluation--Methodology," "Evaluation Research Responsibil-
ities," and "Research in Progress."
      The second section lists additional, unannotated
sources under the same headings. There are no indexes.

225.  Davidson, Claud M. Rural and Suburban Towns:
      Spatial Characteristics of Change in Population and
      Functional Structure. Exchange Bibliography, no.
      272. Monticello, IL: Council of Planning Librarians,
      1972. 18p.
      Books and articles, without restriction as to publi-
cation date, are included in this selected bibliography. "Although emphasizing the spatial, or geographic, aspects of
small-town change, the volume contains references to extensive research reported by scholars in many academic disciplines." Also listed are works that discuss methodologies
appropriate for small-town data analysis.
      Entries are arranged by author within a section on
articles and a section on books. There are no indexes.

226.  Davis, Lenwood G. Rural Population Trends: A Sur-
      vey. Exchange Bibliography, no. 1373. Monticello,
      IL: Council of Planning Librarians, 1977. 11p.
      Focusing on the U.S. population shift from urban

to rural areas, this bibliography lists articles, books, U.S.
government documents, and dissertations. Within each of
these sections entries are arranged alphabetically by author.
Most entries were published in the 1960's or 1970's although
a few have earlier publication dates. There are no indexes.

227. Durand-Drouhin, Jean-Louis; Lili-Maria Szwengrub;
     and Ioan Milhailescu. Rural Community Studies in
     Europe: Trends, Selected and Annotated Bibliog-
     raphies, Analyses. Oxford, U.K.: Pergamon
     Press, Vol. 1, 1981, xi + 332p; Vol. 2, 1982, x +
     271p.
     Great Britain, Ireland, Poland, Turkey, Rumania,
France, and Spain are the countries included in Volume 1 of
this bibliographical work. Volume 2 covers the Netherlands,
the Federal Republic of Germany, Hungary, Italy, and Fin-
land. A third volume is anticipated which will include Aus-
tria, Belgium, Bulgaria, Denmark, Greece, the Soviet Union,
and Yugoslavia.
     Each chapter was contributed by a social scientist
from the country reviewed. "Each author was to try to de-
fine the national traditions, originality of the main schools
and, no less important, place these studies in the social and
intellectual context of their realisation."
     Each of the national studies is "divided into four
parts: (1) Trends and development of rural community studies: this is a historical review of the main features and trends
in rural literature in the country considered from 1920 up to
now and an attempt to categorise research work according to
a number of characteristic approaches. (2) Annotated bibliography: a chronological presentation of the most representative works in the field. (3) Analytical Summaries: a detailed analysis of an average of five to seven outstanding
studies on rural communities; and (4) Location map and Summary Information on located studies."

228. Enders, Wayne T.; Patricia M. Poston; and Ronald
     Briggs. Access to Essential Services in a Rural/
     Urban Environment: A Selected Interdisciplinary
     Bibliography. Exchange Bibliography, no. 593.
     Monticello, IL: Council of Planning Librarians,
     1974. 53p.
     "The main purpose of this literature search was to
create a basis from which sound recommendation could be
offered for improving the accessibility of essential services

to residents of rural areas.  The search focuses on improving
access to the more immediate human needs related to physical,
social, and psychological health rather than to capital improvement projects...."
   Included in the bibliography are government documents, books, articles, dissertations, research papers, and
conference proceedings--most of which were published between 1960 and 1972.  The bibliography is organized into the
following subject chapters:  "Location Analysis for Dispersed
Populations," "Demand for Essential Services," "Supply Systems for Essential Services," "Transportation," "Related Issues of Essential Services Utilization," "Planning for Essential
Service Needs," and "Bibliographies on Relevant Topics."
Entries within chapters are by author.  There are no indexes.

229.  Food and Agriculture Organization of the United Na-
      tions. Documentation Center.  Agricultural Cooper-
      ation: Annotated Bibliography; FAO Publications
      and Documents (1945-Sept. 1971).  FAO, 1971.
      112p. + 5p + 155p.
   Agricultural cooperation is broadly defined in this
bibliography to include many documents relating to rural
sociology and development.  The bibliography is computer-
produced and arranged by FAO accession number.  The
bibliographical list is followed by an analytical index that
provides extensive subject access.  There is also an author
index.

230.  Found, William C.  Environment, Migration, and the
      Management of Rural Resources.  Pt. 1:  Rural
      Sociology, Farm Related Decision-Making and the
      Influence of Environment on Behavior.  Pt. 2.:
      Interregional Migration.  Pt. 3.:  Farm Economics,
      Land Use and Spatial Analysis.  Pt. 4.:  Local
      Studies--Canada, Ontario, and the Counties of
      Kent, Essex, Lanark and Renfrew.  Exchange Bib-
      liography, nos. 1143-1146.  Monticello, IL:  Coun-
      cil of Planning Librarians, 1976.  Pt. 1., 60p;
      Pt. 2., 21p; Pt. 3, 42p; Pt. 4., 26p.
   This bibliography was prepared preliminary to the
author's research into the effects of local environments on
migration and agricultural land management in Southern Ontario.  Only Part IV lists material exclusively relating to
Canada; other parts are very broad in their coverage of
the topic.

Included in these related bibliographies are books, articles, Canadian and Ontario government publications, dissertations, theses, and unpublished reports and papers. Most were published after 1950. Arrangement within each bibliography is alphabetical by author.

231. Gill, Dhara S. A Bibliography of Socio-Economic Studies on Rural Alberta, Canada. Exchange Bibliography, nos. 1260-1262. Monticello, IL: Council of Planning Librarians, 1977. 206p.

Extensive in range and scope, this bibliography includes books; dissertations and theses; articles; provincial, regional, and national government documents; reports of commissions and private firms; and unpublished documents of local interest. Publication dates range from the beginning of the century to the mid-1970's.
Entires are arranged alphabetically by author. There are no indexes.

232. Gilles, Jere Lee. The Sociology of Range Management: A Bibliography. CPL Bibliography, no. 87. Chicago: CPL Bibliographies, 1982. 43p.

"The bibliography is limited to articles written in English, French, or Spanish published since 1960. It does not include so-called fugitive literature--government reports, papers given at professional meetings, and other literature not readily available to researchers and planners."
Arrangement is by author within seven categories--the first on general articles and the next six by geographical area. All regions of the world are covered. There are no indexes but after each entry is one or more of twelve subject terms.

233. Goard, Dean S., and Gary Dickinson. Rural British Columbia: A Bibliography of Social and Economic Research. Special Study, no. 5. Vancouver: Faculty of Education, University of British Columbia, 1970. 33p. ED 040 779.

"The bibliography cites social and economic research pertaining to rural British Columbia. Some 286 entries cover research from before 1940 through 1969. Analysis of the entries by date and source of publication precedes the main list of entries, which is arranged alphabetically by author. Separate indexes are included for author, subject, and geographical area." Primary types of materials listed are journal articles, theses, and publications of universities and provincial and federal government agencies.

234.  Gold, John R., and Margaret M. Gold.  The Crofting
      System:  A Selected Bibliography.  Discussion Paper in Geography, no. 10.  [Oxford, U.K.]:  Oxford Polytechnic, 1979.  33p.
          Over 400 citations, published between 1959 and
      1979, are arranged in one list by author.  The bibliography includes works from several disciplines in the social sciences and humanities.  While historical works are heavily represented, contemporary social studies are also listed to a significant extent.  Books, journal articles, and government and university reports are emphasized in the bibliography; theses, dissertations, and legislation are not included.

235.  Gold, John, and Margaret M. Gold.  Rural Development
      in the Highlands and Islands of Scotland:  A Bibliography.  Public Administration Series, no. P-987.
      Monticello, IL:  Vance Bibliographies, 1982.  28p.
          "The purpose of this bibliography is to bring together the large and disaggregated literature on rural development in the Highlands and Islands of Scotland.  The sources cited span the gambit of the social sciences and humanities as well as including a small number of works which, although intended for the leisure market, manage to supply significant insights into issues of rural development.  We have excluded, however, unpublished theses, official government legislation, and material which appeared in newspapers and journals that have little circulation outside of the region.  In addition, only material published after 1960 is included here, with the exception of a few classic sources from the 1950s."  The bibliography is arranged by author within subject headings such as "Agriculture," "Fishing," "Settlement and Community Life," etc.

236.  Henderson, Francine I., and Johannes B. Opschoor.
      Botswana's Environment:  An Annotated Bibliography.
      Working Bibliography, no. 5.  Gaborone, Botswana:
      National Institute of Development and Cultural Research, [University College of Botswana], 1981.
      v + 83p.
          The majority of entries in this bibliography are UN
      and government documents published in Botswana in the 1960's and 1970's.  The emphasis is on agricultural and

biological research but some items related to rural sociology
are also included.
The bibliography is arranged in one alphabetical
list by author.   In addition to bibliographical information
and an annotation, each citation indicates in which library in
Botswana the item is located.   The bibliography concludes
with a classified subject index and a regional index.

237.  Honadle, Beth Walter.  Public Administration in Rural
       Areas and Small Jurisdictions:  A Guide to the Lit-
       erature.  New York:  Garland, 1983.  xxxi + 146p.
"The purpose of this book is to present a guide to
the literature on public administration in rural areas and
small jurisdictions.   The literature examines characteristics
of small rural communities and shows how those factors affect public service delivery there....   The book has four
main parts:  the largest part being the Bibliography itself.
In addition there are an Introduction, a Directory of National Organizations, an Author index, a Place index, and a Subject index."
       Books, journal articles, government documents, dis-
sertations and theses from 1960 through 1981 are included.
Arrangement is by author within subject chapters and sub-
chapters.   Major subject divisions are "Administration of Human Services," "Administration of Physical Services," "Development," "Government Management and Administration,"
and "Government Organization and Service Delivery."

238.   Human Services in Rural Areas.  Human Services Bib-
       liography Series.  Rockville, MD:  Project SHARE,
       Dept. of Health and Human Services, 1981.  v + 33p.
       Selected and extensively annotated, this bibliography
provides a partial listing of sources owned by Project SHARE.
"The bibliography is divided into three sections:  the abstracts, which are arranged in alphabetical order by author;
an alphabetical list of personal or corporate authors; and an
index of titles.   The abstracts are preceded by citation data
to aid in the identification and ordering of documents."
       A wide range of documents is included.  "The Proj-
ect SHARE bibliography examines the problems and the ad-
vantages of human services delivery in rural areas and reports on programs that have successfully used the positive
elements of rural life to overcome the negative factors.   While
many of the documents concern mental health services, abstracts on rural law enforcement, zoning regulation, medical
care, and services to the elderly are also included."

239. Ilunga, Z.; C. Kangulu; and S.A. Kean. Bibliography
     of Rural Studies Undertaken in Zambia. Chilanga,
     Zambia: Library, Mount Makulu Research Station,
     1983. vii + 133p.
       This bibliography is organized by province, within
     which there is a section on items located within Zambia and
     a smaller section on items identified but not found within
     Zambian institutions. Location information is provided for
     items located within Zambia.
       The bibliography is not limited by type or date of
     publication. It begins with a subject index.

240. International Labour Organization. ILO Publications of
     Interest to Rural Workers: A Bibliography. D.l.1977.
     Geneva: Rural Employment Policies Branch, ILO,
     1977. 92p. Supplement, 1979. 35p.
       "This bibliography has been established with a view
     to enabling the easy retrieval of ILO publications relating to
     problems of rural and plantation workers, indigenous and
     tribal populations, as well as nomads. Even though it may
     not be exhaustive, it roughly covers the past 23 years and
     is concerned with such aspects of rural development as rural
     institutions (excepting co-operatives), rural employment, rural
     vocational training, small-scale industries and the living and
     working conditions of non-urban populations generally."
       The bibliography is organized into 29 chapters by
     type of ILO publication--Committee Reports, articles pub-
     lished in International Labour Review, etc. Within chapters
     arrangement is chronological. Chapter 30 provides a subject
     index.

241. Lassanyi, Mary E. Agriculture in Central America
     1970-1983: 153 Citations. Quick Bibliography
     Series. no. 84-04. Beltsville, MD: National Agri-
     cultural Library, 1983. 14p. + 8p.
       Unavailable for annotation.

242. Lassanyi, Mary E. Social, Structural, and Technologi-
     cal Changes in Agriculture. Quick Bibliography
     Series, no. 84-39. Beltsville, MD: National Agri-
     cultural Library, 1984. 27p.
       The 222 citations to English language publications
     in this bibliography result from a computer search of the
     Agricola data base. The bibliography covers the period
     from 1979 to March 1984 and updates an earlier bibliography

of the same title. The format of the bibliography is a reproduction of the print-out. There is a concluding author index.

243. Lefaver, Scott, and Nancy Koenig. Rural Planning
     Bibliography. Exchange Bibliography, no. 1505.
     Monticello, IL: Council of Planning Librarians,
     1978. 8p.
     This is a partially annotated bibliography of items
published, with a few exceptions, in the 1970's. Included
are articles, books, pamphlets, and government publications
dealing with rural planning in the U.S. in general or with
California specifically.
     The bibliography is divided into the following sec-
tions: "Rural Land Use Planning," "Rural Living," "Agricultural Land Use Planning," "Mixed Land Use Planning,"
"Agricultural/Rural Planning--California," and "Agricultural/
Rural Planning--Santa Clara County, California." Within
sections entries are arranged alphabetically by author.
There are no indexes.

244. Link, Albert D. Rural Education and Small Schools, A
     Selected Bibliography (with ERIC abstracts). Sup-
     plement No. 2. Las Cruces: Educational Resources
     Information Center, Clearinghouse on Rural Educa-
     tion and Small Schools, New Mexico State University,
     1972. 379p. ED 065 256.
     "Documents relating to rural education and small
schools are cited in this bibliography. A supplement to 2
previous ERIC/CRESS publications: 'Rural Education and
Small Schools, A Selected Bibliography' (ED 033 257) and
'Rural Education and Small Schools, A Selected Bibliography
--Supplement No. 1' (ED 055 695), the present bibliography
contains 267 citations and abstracts which have appeared in
'Current Index to Journals in Education' from January 1971
through March 1972. Major emphasis is placed on rural education, rural development, and rural-urban differences. Subject indexes and ordering information are appended."

245. Lutes, Terry. Rural Political Behavior. Public Admin-
     istration Series, no. P-717. Monticello, IL: Vance
     Bibliographies, 1981. 14p.
     This bibliography is restricted to the United States
but is not limited by either date of publication or discipline.
Included are "nearly 200 selected works having to do with
the political activity, or sociological and economic basis for
that activity, of rural citizens."

246. Luzuriaga, Carlos C., and Clarence Zuvekas. An An-
     notated Bibliography of Income, Income Distribution,
     and Levels of Living in Rural Ecuador. Ecuador,
     General Working Document, no. 1. [Washington,
     D.C.]: Rural Development Division, Bureau for
     Latin America and the Caribbean, [U.S.] Agency
     for International Development, 1979. 97p.
         Nearly 700 works in English or Spanish are ar-
     ranged in one alphabetical list by author. With a few ex-
     ceptions citations are to works published after 1950. Books,
     journal articles, theses, dissertations, and other published
     and unpublished research reports are included. There is
     an index by province and an index by subject.

247. Management of Agriculture:  A Selected Bibliography.
     Occasional Bibliography, no. 1. Kuala Lumpur,
     [Malaysia]: Library, Asian Centre for Development
     Administration, 1976. 19p.
         "This bibliography contains over 100 selected partly
     annotated references on Agricultural Policy, Planning, Imple-
     mentation and Management. The references listed include
     books, articles, reports and conference papers." Arrange-
     ment is by author within the four subject categories. Al-
     most all citations are to works published in the 1960's or
     1970's.

248. McHenry, Dean E. Ujamaa Villages in Tanzania:  A
     Bibliography. Uppsala, Sweden: Scandinavian
     Institute of African Studies, 1981. 69p.
         "The most ambitious effort of any African country
     to initiate the establishment of a socialist society is Tanzania's
     attempt to create ujamaa villages. This is a bibliography of
     books, articles and papers on the subject published up to
     1980. Most of the materials are in English, several are in
     Swahili, some in French, a few in German and still fewer in
     other languages. The works are organized by their dominant
     theme into sections within four basic subject categories: the
     evolution, formation, character and evaluation of ujamaa vil-
     lages or efforts to build ujamaa villages. An author and a
     subject index are included...."

249. Moore, Mick; John Connell; and Claire M. Lambert.
     Village Studies Data Analysis and Bibliography.
     Vol. 1, India, 1950-1975; Vol. 2, Africa, Middle
     East and North Africa, Asia (excluding India),

Pacific Islands, Latin America, West Indies and the
Caribbean, 1950-1975. London: Mansell, Vol. 1,
1976; Vol. 2, 1978. 319p.

Produced by the staff at the Institute of Development Studies at the University of Sussex, these two volumes
reflect the Institute's efforts in "evaluating and analyzing
village studies undertaken in poor countries since 1950."
About 3,000 studies were identified, about half of them were
done in India.

Volume I was unavailable for annotation. Citations
to the studies in Volume II are arranged by country and
author. Each citation has a narrative annotation. Additionally, the studies have all been analyzed and for those with
data on a wide range of variables, a coded statement on the
kinds of data presented in the study appears next to the citation.

There is a concluding topics index and author index.

250. Muenkner, H. Annotated Bibliography on Cooperatives
and Rural Poverty. Food and Agriculture Organization, 1978.
Unavailable for annotation.

251. Nakhjvani, Mehran. Agrarian Reform in Latin America:
The Role of Marketing and Credit; An Annotated
Bibliography. Bibliography Series, no. 6. Mon-
treal: Centre for Developing-Area Studies, 1977.
46p.

Books, periodical articles, government and UN documents, theses, dissertations, unpublished papers, and conference proceedings, almost all published since 1970, have
been selected and partially annotated for this bibliography.

The bibliography is organized into general works
on agrarian reform, selected country studies on agrarian reform, and then several chapters relating to agricultural credit and cooperatives. Within chapters and sub-chapters arrangement is alphabetical by author.

Appendices provide information on sources, a glossary of acronyms, and a list of useful journals. There is an
author index and a country index.

252. National Institute of Community Development. Agricul-
ture and Food Production in India: A Bibliography.
Hyderabad, [India]: The Institute, 1971. 151p.
The majority of the 2,378 citations in this bibliography

are to Indian journal articles and monographs published between 1960 and 1970.   While agricultural and economic aspects of food production are emphasized, materials on social
aspects of Indian agriculture are also included under subject
headings such as "Cooperative Farming," "Community Development and Panchayati Raj," "Agricultural Labor," and
"Agrarian Unrest."
     The bibliography is organized into several subject
chapters within which entries are arranged alphabetically by
author. There are no indexes.

253. Neate, Simon.  Rural Deprivation:  An Annotated Bib-
          liography of Economic and Social Problems in Rural
          Britain.  GEO Abstracts Bibliography, no. 8.  Nor-
          wich, U.K.:  GEO Abstracts, 1981.  81p.
     "The annotated bibliography consists of references
to research, analysis and comment on the general topic of
disadvantage in the rural areas of Great Britain, and, more
commonly, particular aspects of it which have appeared in
the form of books, semi-published reports and papers, and
articles and papers in national serials in the English language." Ninety percent of the items included were published in the 1970's.
     The bibliography is organized into two sections--
"Underlying Issues" and "Economic and Social Problems of
Rural Areas." These are further divided into subject sub-
sections, within which arrangement is chronological.  Cross-
references are provided at the beginning of each sub-section.
There is an author index and a geographical index.

254. Newman, Bobbie G.  Rural Nonfarm Population:  A
          Guide to the Literature.  Public Administration
          Series, no. P-418.  Monticello, IL:  Vance Bibliog-
          raphies, 1980.  20p.
     The U.S. rural nonfarm population lives in the un-
incorporated fringe of smaller urban areas, in isolated nonfarm homes, or in communities of fewer than 2,500.  The
compiler has provided a list of relevant references including
books, periodical articles, government documents, and dissertations and other unpublished papers.  The bibliography
is not limited by date of publication and concludes with an
annotated list of literature consulted.

255. Organisation for Economic Co-operation and Develop-
          ment.  Development Centre.  Agricultural Co-

operatives: Annotated Bibliography. Paris: The
Organisation, 1971. 194p.
This selected bibliography provides lengthy annotations of "books and articles, records of congresses and
meetings, as well as F.A.O. and other documents." Most of
the citations are to works published in the 1960's. Not all
are to English language publications.
The first two chapters list general works on agricultural co-operatives and agricultural co-operatives in developing countries. Chapter III provides references to studies
classified by groups of countries--i.e., developing countries,
Israel, socialist countries, and free market economies. Within
chapters arrangement is alphabetical by author. There are
no indexes.

256. Ouedrago, Ismael; Mark D. Newman; and David W.
      Norman. The Farmer in the Semi-Arid Tropics of
      West Africa: A Partially Annotated Bibliography.
      Research Bulletin, vol. 2, no. 4. Patancheru,
      India: International Crops Research Institute for
      the Semi-Arid Tropics, 1982. ix + 122p.
      "This is a partially annotated bibliography of formal-
ly and semi-formally published documents on socioeconomic
aspects of farm and village production systems in the semi-
arid tropics of West Africa.... A total of 1045 references
are included, 561 of them with annotations from various
sources. Most of them are dated from 1960 to 1980...."
      Arrangement is by author under each of the ten
countries (Benin, Cameroon, Chad, Gambia, Ghana, Mali,
Niger, Nigeria, Senegal, and Upper Volta) and under a
"General" chapter. Each entry has been assigned one or
more numbers referring to a classified subject index which
appears at the end of the bibliography along with an author
index. Both French and English language publications are
included in the bibliography.

257. Parker, J. Kathy, and Joyce K. Berry. The Social
      and Environmental Consequences of Current Trends
      of Non-Metro Growth: An Annotated Bibliography.
      New Haven, CT: School of Forestry and Environ-
      mental Studies, Yale University, 1979. 152p.
      NTIS, PB80-182561.
      The annotated bibliography portion of this work is
found between pages 10 and 90. The emphasis of the bibliography is on journal articles and papers presented to the

annual meeting of the Rural Sociology Society. The bibliography is limited to research in the U.S. from 1974 through
1979. There are no indexes but there are several appendices
providing information on the compilers' methodology, as well
as such information as a list of researchers to contact on
specific issues.

258.  Philippine Council for Agriculture and Resources Re-
      search. Bibliography of Studies in Socio-Economics,
      1976-1978. Los Baños, Laguna, Philippines: Socio-
      Economics Research Division, The Council, 1979.
      99p.
      Intended to update a 1976 publication, this bibliog-
raphy includes theses, dissertations, conference proceedings,
journal articles, and research publications of Philippine universities, institutes, and government departments.
      Part I is devoted to agricultural economics; Part II
to applied rural sociology. In Part II works are arranged by
author within 12 categories: agrarian reform, agricultural
education, communications, community development, ethno-
cultural communities, extension education, agricultural financing, manpower, rural development, sociological organization,
sociology, and sociological data base. There are no indexes.

259.  Poole, Dennis L. Rural Social Welfare: Educators and
      Practitioners. New York: Praeger, 1981. xi +
      317p.
      Included in this annotated bibliography are govern-
ment documents, books, journal articles, and ERIC documents.
Most entries date from the late 1960's although a few have
publication dates from as early as the 1940's. Chapters are
organized by subject areas common to social work curricula.
The first five chapters cover general topics--human behavior
in the rural social environment; rural social research, rural
social policy, rural human services; and planning, administration and community development in rural areas. The next
four chapters are on specific areas of concern to rural social
welfare--health, mental health, children and youth, and aging.
The last chapter lists curriculum materials for rural social
work education.
      When appropriate, entries are listed in more than
one chapter. Arrangement within chapters is alphabetical by
title. There is an author index.

260.  Ranasinghe, W.; S.M.K. Mileham; and C. Gunatunga.

A Bibliography of Socio-Economic Studies in the
Agrarian Sector of Sri Lanka. Colombo, Sri Lanka:
Agrarian Research & Training Institute, 1977. v +
208p.

While much of this bibliography is devoted to agricultural and economic aspects of rural life in Sri Lanka,
works in rural sociology are also included. The bibliography
includes a wide range of published and unpublished materials,
not limited by date. All citations are to materials located in
institutions in Sri Lanka. The bibliography is organized into
subject chapters within which arrangement is alphabetical by
author. There are no indexes.

261. Ray, William W. The Rural-Urban Fringe. Exchange
     Bibliography, no. 133. Monticello, IL: Council of
     Planning Librarians, 1970. 8p.

Included in this bibliography are books, articles,
conference proceedings, government documents, theses and
dissertations from the 1940's through the 1960's. Entries
represent the disciplines of planning, geography, sociology,
and economics and are arranged by author. There are no
indexes.

262. Richeson, Meg. Canadian Rural Sociology Bibliography.
     Exchange Bibliography, no. 238. Monticello, IL:
     Council of Planning Librarians, 1971. 58p.

Intended for support of a university-level course,
this bibliography includes government documents, books,
theses, dissertations, reports, symposium papers, articles,
films, and paintings from the beginning of the century through
the 1960's.

The bibliography does not include "natural resource
development (fishing, hunting, logging), recreational development, and many studies of rural life among ethnic, racial, or
religious minorities. Included in the bibliography are items
on demography (migration, settlement, stratification), and
levels of rural living, rural history, rural and regional development, rural poverty, rural institutions (government,
education, welfare), and rural organizations. Most of the
borderline items between rural sociology and agricultural
economics, especially those dealing with production or statistical methodology and research methods, have also been
excluded."

The bibliography is organized by type of material--
monographs, articles, bibliographies, films, and paintings.

Within each section entries are arranged by author. There
are no indexes.

263. Rural Education, A Selected Bibliography (with ERIC
     abstracts). Las Cruces: Educational Resources
     Information Center, Clearinghouse on Rural Educa-
     tion and Small Schools, New Mexico State University,
     1974. 453p. ED 097 186.
     "Documents relating to rural education are cited in
this annotated bibliography. The 335 citations and abstracts
appeared in 'Research in Education' (RIE) from April 1973
through June 1974. Also included are 149 citations which appeared in 'Current Index to Journals in Education' (CIJE)
from April 1973 through June 1974. Major emphasis is
placed on rural education, rural development, and rural urban differences. A combined RIE and CIJE subject index is
provided at the end of the bibliography...."

264. Rural Education, A Selected Bibliography (with ERIC
     abstracts). Supplement No. 1. Las Cruces: Edu-
     cational Resources Information Center, Clearing-
     house on Rural Education and Small Schools, New
     Mexico State University, 1975. 298p. ED 107 429.
     This bibliography contains 196 citations from Re-
sources in Education, July 1974 through March 1975 and 106
citations from Current Index to Journals in Education for the
same period. "A wide variety of material (annual reports,
technical reports, books, program descriptions, etc.) is
covered. Subject areas most frequently cited include: rural
youth, rural urban differences, rural development, migration
patterns, economic disadvantaged, and developing nations."
There is a subject index.

265. Rural Education, A Selected Bibliography (with ERIC
     abstracts). Supplement No. 2. Las Cruces: Edu-
     cational Resources Information Center, Clearing-
     house on Rural Education and Small Schools, New
     Mexico State University, 1976. 352p. ED 125 808.
     This bibliography supplements six earlier publica-
tions and contains 267 citations from Resources in Education,
April 1975 through March 1976 and 72 citations from Current
Index to Journals in Education for the same period.
     "A wide variety of material (annual reports, techni-
cal reports, books, program descriptions, etc.) is covered.
Subject areas most frequently cited include: rural develop-

ment, rural schools, small schools, rural population, rural urban differences, rural areas, program descriptions, and developing nations." There is a subject index.

266. Rural Education, A Bibliography of ERIC Abstracts. Supplement No. 3. Las Cruces: Educational Resources Information Center, Clearinghouse on Rural Education and Small Schools, New Mexico State University, 1977. 257p. ED 144 772.

This supplement includes 180 citations from Resources in Education from April 1976 through May 1977 and 79 citations from Current Index to Journals in Education for the same period.

"Subject areas most frequently cited in this bibliography include: vocational education; adult education; developing nations; program descriptions; program guides; rural development; rural education, rural areas; rural population; rural schools, rural urban differences; rural youth, and World Congress of Rural Sociology." There is a subject index.

267. Rural Education and Small Schools, A Selected Bibliography (with ERIC Abstracts). Supplement No. 3. Las Cruces: Educational Resources Information Center, Clearinghouse on Rural Education and Small Schools, New Mexico State University, 1973. 312p. ED 081 532.

This bibliography supplements previous ERIC bibliographies. Listed are citations and abstracts appearing in Resources in Education and Current Index to Journals in Education from April 1972 through March 1973. There is a subject index.

268. Rural Population Change in New Zealand: A Bibliography of Manuscripts Written Between 1960-1980. Studies in Rural Change, no. 5. Edited by Richard Bedford. Christchurch, New Zealand: [Dept. of Geography, University of Canterbury], 1980. viii + 211p.

Over 900 items are included in this extensive bibliography, the first part of which is organized into three subject chapters: "Population Dynamics," "Population Characteristics," and "Settlement Dynamics." The next sections arrange the citations first by geographical region, then by type of publication (General references and bibliographies,

Unpublished theses, Journal articles, Chapters in Books,
Central and local government reports, Research reports [non-
government] and Conference papers), and lastly in one complete alphabetical list. There are no indexes.

269.  Sauquet, Michel.  Selected Bibliography on Socio-
      Economic Features of Rural Ethiopia.  Addis Ababa:
      Institute of Development Research in collaboration
      with Agriservice Ethiopia, 1977.  iii + 65 pages.
      This bibliography lists "560 selected titles, all of
them related to socio-economic problems in rural areas.  The
list concentrates on literature published over the past ten
years (1966-1976), with a special concern in the publications
of the post-revolutionary period (1974-1976) which account
for more than one third of the mentioned titles."
      A wide variety of materials is included in the bibli-
ography; most are in English, although Amharic, French,
and German are also represented.  The bibliography is divided into thirteen headings:  "Demography," "Sociology,"
"Women," "Politics," "Law," "Economy," "Agriculture," "Land
Reform," "Rural Development," "Field Surveys," "Marketing,"
"Education," and "Health."  There is an author index and an
appendix listing "Addis Ababa Special Libraries that could be
of Assistance to Ethiopian Socio-Economic Development Research."

270.  Schatzberg, Michael G.  Bibliography of Small Urban
      Centers in Rural Development in Africa.  Madison:
      African Studies Program, University of Wisconsin,
      1979.  ix + 246p.
      Over 2,000 citations are listed to works in French
or English, most of which were published in the 1960's to
mid-1970's.  Books, journal articles, dissertations, theses,
and other published and unpublished research papers are
included.  "For the purposes of this bibliographic search, a
small urban center was arbitrarily defined as a town with a
present-day population of 2,000-50,000."  Exceptions at both
ends of the scale were sometimes made.
      The bibliography is organized by country and then
by author.  There is both an author index and a subject
index.

271.  Schweri, William F.  Bibliography of Appalachian Stud-
      ies, CDC Development Paper, no. 4.  Lexington:
      Center for Developmental Change, University of
      Kentucky, 1973.  30p.  ED 082 879.

"Studies of various aspects of Appalachian life are listed in this 396-item bibliography. Works are listed alphabetically by author and include journal articles, books, conference proceedings, theses and dissertations. The selections cover the period 1930-1972 with examples from each decade."

272.  Shah, Makhdoom A., et al.  Annotated Bibliography on: Rural Poverty and Employment, Internal Migration, Agriculture, Mechanization and Employment, Rural Manpower Development, International Migration, Resettlement of Returning Migrants. Islamabad, Pakistan: Pakistan Manpower Institute, 1978. iv + 200p.
      This is an extensive listing of over 1,000 items related to the subjects listed in the title. Entries are not limited by publication type, date, place, or language; although the majority of items were published in English in the 1960's or 1970's. Included are works relating to countries in both the developing and the developed world.
      The bibliography is organized into the indicated six subject chapters, within which arrangement is alphabetical by author. There is both a geographical and a subject index, the latter being organized by specific terms within the subject areas used to organize the bibliography.

273.  Sharma, Prakash C.  Selected Bibliography on Small Town Research. Exchange Bibliography, no. 713. Monticello, IL: Council of Planning Librarians, 1974. 12p.
      This selected list of government documents, books, articles, reports, theses, and dissertations includes some items dating from the last century, but most of the citations are to works published between 1920 and 1971. There are two sections; one on monographs, the other on articles. Within each section the entries are arranged by author. There are no indexes.

274.  68 Micro-level Studies: Abstract Reports on Rural Problems and Development. Bangladesh: Civil Officers' Training Academy, 1980. 70p.
      Unavailable for annotation.

275.  Smith, Suzanne M.  An Annotated Bibliography of Small Town Research. Madison: Dept. of Rural Sociology, College of Agricultural and Life Sciences,

University of Wisconsin, 1970. vii + 137 leaves.
ED 042 562.

"The purpose of this bibliography is to bring together books, articles and bulletins which have been written
from 1900 to 1968 on small towns in the United States. Particular attention has been given to works with a demographic
or ecological perspective."
The bibliography is organized into four sections.
The first is "Books, Articles, and Bulletins on the Small
Town," the second is "Theses on the Small Town," and the
last two list related works. The bibliography next lists other
bibliographies. Within sections arrangement is alphabetical
by author. There is a limited subject index that classifies
all entries into one of six categories: "Problems and Policy,"
"National Patterns of Growth and Decline," "Factors Associ-
ated with Growth and Decline," "The Village as a Rural
Trade Center," "Town-Country Relations," and "Types of
Villages and Economic Functions."

276.  Steer, Edgar S.  A Select Bibliography of Reference
      Material Providing an Introduction to the Study of
      Jamaican Agriculture.  Kingston, Jamaica:  Agricul-
      tural Planning Unit, Ministry of Agriculture and
      Fisheries, 1970.  40p.
      While much of this work is concerned with technical,
historical, and economic aspects of Jamaican agriculture, sections on "Agricultural Policy," "Sociology," "Land Use," etc.
do provide citations to rural sociological studies.  There is
no restriction by type or date of publication.

277.  Taylor, E. Barbara.  Land, Agriculture and the Family
      Farm; Selected Material in the California State Li-
      brary.  ALR Special Bibliography, no. 1.  Sacra-
      mento:  Administrative-Legislative Reference, Cal-
      ifornia State Library, 1977.  17p. + 4p.
      State and federal documents, periodical articles,
and books, almost all of which were published since 1970,
are included in this bibliography.  Organized under twelve
subject headings, the bibliography emphasizes but by no
means limits itself to titles concerned with agriculture in
California.
      Entries are arranged by author under subject head-
ings.  There are no indexes.  The bibliography concludes
with a four-page supplement dated December 1977.

278.  Teweldeberhan Zerom.  A Selected and Annotated Bib-
      liography on Socio-Economic Rural Research in
      Ethiopia.  Addis Ababa:  Institute of Development
      Research, 1974.  17 leaves.
         This extensively annotated but brief bibliography
      lists books, research reports, and government and UN docu-
      ments.  All items included can be found in Ethiopian librar-
      ies.  Inclusion is not restricted by date of publication.

279.  Thirsk, Wayne R.  A Selective Annotated Bibliography
      of Rural Poverty in Colombia.  Colombia, Working
      Document, no. 1.  [Washington, D.C.]:  Rural De-
      velopment Division, Bureau for Latin America and
      the Caribbean, [U.S.] Agency for International
      Development, 1977.  11p.
         "A great deal of scholarly attention has been fo-
      cussed on the performance of the rural sector in Colombia
      since 1950.  This bibliography describes what is considered
      to be the most comprehensive or thorough of the numerous
      attempts to assess this performance....  Each of the studies
      listed here has built upon the foundation laid down by earlier
      investigations and incorporated many of their results.  As a
      general rule of thumb, the more recent is the date of the
      cited work the more likely the reader will be to find exten-
      sive reference to its predecessors.  Besides the references
      to analyses of rural income, price and employment data, this
      bibliography contains citations of the primary data sources
      that have provided most of the grist for the analytical work
      that has been done on Colombia."

280.  Tremblay, Kenneth R.  Objective Quality of Life in
      Rural America:  A Selected Bibliography.  Public
      Administration Series, no. P-905.  Monticello, IL:
      Vance Bibliographies, 1982.  8p.
         "The literature contained in this bibliography is cate-
      gorized into eight major quality of life components:  General
      quality of life issues, income and employment, education,
      community services, health care, housing, crime, and family
      concerns.
         "The publications were selected to represent the
      range of theoretical thinking and research efforts conducted
      on objective rural quality of life in the past decade.  An
      emphasis has been placed on more recent publications...."
      Monographs, journal articles and government publications
      are all included.

281. Tremblay, Kenneth R. Perceived Quality of Life in
     Rural America: A Selective Bibliography. Public
     Administration Series, no. P-759. Monticello, IL:
     Vance Bibliographies, 1981. 8p.
     The journal articles, monographs, and government
     documents selected for this bibliography all address the is-
     sue of perceived quality of life in rural United States. "The
     publications are selected to represent the range of theoreti-
     cal thinking and research efforts conducted on the topic in
     recent years--namely 1970-1980."

282. Truong, Thanh-Dam. Small-Scale Farming: A Selected
     and Annotated Bibliography with Emphasis on South
     East Asia and West Africa. The Hague: Institute
     of Social Studies, 1978. v + 68p. Rev. ed., 1980.
     vii + 98p.
     This bibliography was originally developed in con-
     junction with a seminar on "The future viability of small-
     scale farming" held at the Institute of Social Studies in 1978.
     Items listed "are limited to books, documents, conference
     papers and reports written in the English and French lan-
     guages available at the library of the Institute of Social
     Studies." The bibliography is arranged in one list by au-
     thor. There is a subject index and a geographical index.

283. Tschiersch, Joachim E. Cooperation in Agricultural
     Production. Publications of the Research Centre
     for International Agrarian Development, vol 3.
     Saarbrücken, W. Germany: Verlag der SSIP-
     Schriften Breitenbach, 1976. 188p.
     "The term 'cooperation in agricultural production,'
     as used in the present bibliography, covers the various ar-
     rangements between farmers for cooperative or joint action
     in the production process itself. It thus does not cover co-
     operative activities in the stages prior to or following pro-
     duction, such as credit, supply and marketing. Cooperation
     in agricultural production can range from informal types of
     mutual assistance in certain operations to complex systems of
     joint management which involve the pooling of all the produc-
     tion resources of the cooperating farmers."
          The main purpose of the bibliography is to provide
     a listing of the holdings in the collection on cooperation in
     agricultural production in the Research Centre for Interna-
     tional Agrarian Development. These items are marked with a
     "+". Additional important items are also included. Listing

works representing a variety of European languages, the bibliography covers all areas of the world except for socialist
Eastern Europe.

284.  Turner, P.V.  "Rural Malawi:  An Approach to a Cur-
      rent Bibliography," Rural Africana 21 (Summer
      1973):59-66.
In this bibliographical essay the author includes
works from several disciplines within the social sciences.
Books, journal articles, government reports, final year seminar papers from students at the University of Malawi, and
research in progress are all included without limitation by
date.

285.  University of Wisconsin.  Land Tenure Center Library.
      Agrarian Reform in Brazil:  A Bibliography (Part 1).
      Training & Methods Series, no. 18.  Madison:  Land
      Tenure Center Library, 1972.  91p.  Supplement,
      1977.  51p.
This bibliography lists relevant holdings in the Land
Tenure Center Library.  The majority of references are to
works in Portuguese.  Arrangement is by author under numerous subject headings--e.g., "Agrarian Reform and Land
Tenure," "Labor," and "Population Studies."  A call number
or other indication of location within the Library is provided
for each item.  There are no indexes.

286.  University of Wisconsin.  Land Tenure Center Library.
      Agrarian Reform in Brazil (Part II:  Regional De-
      velopment).  Training & Methods Series, no. 19.
      Madison:  Land Tenure Center Library, 1972.  57p.
This bibliography of relevant holdings in the Land
Tenure Center Library is organized by region within which
there is a further division by "agriculture," "economic affairs," and "social affairs."  Introductory information indicates the states included in each region.  Most works listed
are in Portuguese.  A call number or other indication of location within the Library is provided for each item.  There
are no indexes.

287.  University of Wisconsin.  Land Tenure Center Library.
      The Central American Agrarian Economy:  A Bibli-
      ography (Part I:  Regional, Belize, Costa Rica, El
      Salvador).  Training & Methods Series, no. 26.
      Madison:  Land Tenure Center Library, 1975.  97p.

This bibliography lists holdings related to Central
America in the Land Tenure Center Library.  Broader in
coverage than subjects related to rural sociology and including primarily works in Spanish, it is included here because
of its listings of works on agrarian reform and land tenure.
After a section on the region as a whole, the bibliography is arranged by country, within which there are
further subject sub-divisions.  The bibliography is not limited by date or type of publication.  As with other bibliographies in this series, each entry has been given a call number or other location designation within the Land Tenure Center Library.  There are no indexes.

288.    University of Wisconsin.  Land Tenure Center Library.
        The Central American Agrarian Economy:  A Bibli-
        ography (Part II:  Guatemala, Honduras, Nicaragua,
        Panama).  Training & Methods Series, no. 27.
        Madison:  Land Tenure Center Library, 1978.  98p.
        Similar to Part I, Part II covers different geographi-
cal areas.

289.    University of Wisconsin.  Land Tenure Center Library.
        Chile's Agricultural Economy:  A Bibliography.
        Training & Methods Series, no. 12.  Madison:  Land
        Tenure Center Library, 1970.  65p.  Supplement
        no. 1, 1971.  20p.  Supplement no. 2, 1974.  37p.
        Relevant holdings of the Land Tenure Center Library
are listed by author under subject headings and sub-headings.
The five major subject divisions are "General," "Agriculture,"
"Economy," "Politics & Law," and "Society."  The bibliography
is not restricted by type or date of publication; most of the
references are to Spanish language publications.  A call number or other location information within the Land Tenure Center Library is provided for each item.  There are no indexes.

290.    University of Wisconsin.  Land Tenure Center Library.
        Colombia:  Background and Trends--A Bibliography.
        Training & Methods Series, no. 9.  Madison:  Land
        Tenure Center Library, 1969.  56p.  Supplement
        no. 1, 1971.  34p.  Supplement no. 2, 1973.  34p.
        While this bibliography and its supplements do not
deal exclusively with works related to rural sociology or primarily with works in English, they are included because of
their strong section on agrarian reform and land tenure.
        The supplements are arranged in one alphabetical

list by author. The original bibliography is arranged by author within subject headings and sub-headings. The major headings are "General," "Agriculture," "Economy," "Politics," and "Society." There is no limitation by date or type of publication. All relevant materials from the Land Tenure Center Library are included. A call number or other information concerning location within the Land Tenure Center Library is given for each item. There are no indexes.

291. University of Wisconsin. Land Tenure Center Library. East & Southeast Asia: A Bibliography. Training & Methods Series, no. 14. Madison: Land Tenure Center Library, 1971. 88p. Supplement no. 1, 1972. 46p. Supplement no. 2, 1979. 119p. Supplement no. 3, 1980. 71p.

This extensive bibliography lists citations to all holdings in the Land Tenure Center Library relating to East and Southeast Asia. While by no means limited to rural sociology or related topics, works on rural or agricultural development, land tenure and use, and rural manpower are a substantial part of the bibliography.

The bibliography is organized by country and by author. Supplements 2 and 3 include subject divisions under each country. Supplements 2 and 3 must be used together for a complete geographical coverage. Supplement 2 includes China, Hong Kong, Japan, Korea, Macao, and Taiwan. Supplement 3 covers Burma, Cambodia, Indonesia, Laos, Malaysia, and the Pacific Ocean Islands.

Neither the bibliography nor the supplements have indexes. A call number or other information concerning location within the Land Tenure Center Library is provided for each item.

292. University of Wisconsin. Land Tenure Center Library. Economic Aspects of Agricultural Development in Ecuador: A Bibliography. Training & Methods Series, no. 21. Madison: Land Tenure Center Library, 1972. 28p.

Arranged under 19 subject headings, this bibliography lists relevant holdings of the Land Tenure Center Library. The subject of economic aspects of agricultural development is broadly defined, and subject divisions include "agrarian reform," "land tenure," "social affairs," etc. Spanish language publications predominate. The bibliography is not restricted by type or date of publication. A call

number or other indication of location within the Land Tenure
Center Library is provided for each item.

293.  University of Wisconsin.  Land Tenure Center Library.
      Land Tenure and Agrarian Reform in Mexico--A
      Bibliography.  Training & Methods Series, no. 10.
      Madison:  Land Tenure Center Library, 1970.  51p.
      Supplement no. 1, [1971?].  Supplement no. 2, 1976,
      67p.
      While this bibliography and its supplement do not
deal exclusively with works in English related to rural sociology, they are included here because of their strong sections on agrarian reform and land tenure.
      The supplement is arranged in one alphabetical list
by author.  The original bibliography is arranged by author
within subject headings and sub-headings.  The major headings are "General," "Agriculture," "Economy," "Politics,"
and "Society."  There is no limitation by date or type of
publication.  All relevant holdings of the Land Tenure Center Library are included and each item is given a call number or other information concerning location within the Land
Tenure Center Library.  The supplement concludes with a
subject index.

294.  University of Wisconsin.  Land Tenure Center Library.
      Near East & South Asia:  A Bibliography.  Training
      & Methods Series, no. 13.  Madison:  Land Tenure
      Center Library, 1971.  74p.  Supplement, no. 1,
      1972.  Supplement, no. 2, 1976.  99p.
      This extensive bibliography lists citations to all
holdings in the Land Tenure Center Library relating to the
Near East and South Asia.  While by no means limited to
rural sociology or related topics, works on rural and agricultural development, land tenure and use, and rural manpower are a substantial part of the bibliography.
      The bibliography is not restricted by type or date
of publication and is arranged by country and author.  In
the supplements there are subject divisions under most countries.  There are no indexes.  A call number or other information concerning location within the Land Tenure Center Library is provided for each item.

295.  University of Wisconsin.  Land Tenure Center Library.
      Peru, Land & People--A Bibliography.  Training
      & Methods Series, no. 15.  Madison:  Land Tenure

Center Library, 1971. 71p. Supplement, 1972.
20p. Supplement, no. 2, 1980. 73p.
This is a bibliography of materials dealing with
Peru that are in the Land Tenure Center Library. While
the majority of works listed are in Spanish and the bibliography is not limited to works related to rural sociology, it
is included here because of its coverage of agrarian reform,
land tenure, and related subjects.
The original bibliography is arranged by author
within subject headings and sub-headings. The five major
subject headings are "General," "Agriculture," "Economics,"
"Politics and Government," and "Social Conditions." Supplement 1 is a straight alphabetical list by author while Supplement 2 has some variation in subject headings from the original bibliography.
The bibliographies are not restricted by date or
type of publication. There are no indexes. A call number
or other information providing location within the Land Tenure Center Library is provided for each item.

296.  University of Wisconsin. Land Tenure Center Library.
      Rural Development in Africa: A Bibliography (Part I:
      General, Central, East). Training & Methods Series,
      no. 16. Madison: Land Tenure Center Library, 1971.
      83p. Supplement, 1973. 104p. Supplement no. 2,
      1974. 94p.
      This bibliography lists material on Africa in the
Land Tenure Center Library. The introductory general
section is arranged by author within subject headings, e.g.,
agriculture, economic affairs, human resources, etc. The
other sections are arranged by country, sometimes with subject divisions.
      There is no restriction by date or type of publica-
tion. There are no indexes. Each entry notes the call number or other location information for the Land Tenure Center
Library.

297.  University of Wisconsin. Land Tenure Center Library.
      Rural Development in Africa: A Bibliography.
      (Part II: North, South, West). Training &
      Methods Series, no. 17. Madison: Land Tenure
      Center Library, 1971. 86p. Supplement no. 1,
      1973. 50p. Supplement no. 2, 1974. 73p.
      Similar to Part I, Part II covers different geograph-
ical areas.

298. University of Wisconsin. Land Tenure Center Library.
     Rural Development in Venezuela and the Guianas:
     A Bibliography. Training & Methods Series, no.
     20. Madison: Land Tenure Center Library, 1972.
     67p. ED 138 417.
     This bibliography presents a listing of relevant
holdings in the Land Tenure Center Library. Divided into
20 subject sections and three geographical sections (French
Guiana, Guyana, and Surinam), the bibliography emphasizes
Spanish language publications and is not restricted by type
or date of publication. A call number or other indication of
location within the Library is provided for each item. There
are no indexes.

299. Wimberly, Ronald C., and Charles N. Bebee. Structure
     of U.S. Agriculture Bibliography. Bibliographies
     and Literature of Agriculture, no. 16. Beltsville,
     MD: Science and Education Administration, U.S.
     Dept. of Agriculture, 1981. v + 514p.
     This is a computer-generated bibliography covering
the years 1970 through 1979. Part I contains citations from
the Agricola data base and Part II lists citations from the
American Agricultural Economics Documentation subfile of
Agricola. The parts are divided into subject chapters, such
as "General Agriculture and Rural Sociology," "Agricultural
Administration and Management," and "Agricultural Policies
and Programs." Within these chapters arrangement is alphabetical by author.
     While much of the bibliography is devoted to litera-
ture in agricultural economics, rural sociology is included to
a significant extent. There are no indexes.

# HEALTH

300. Bender, Deborah, and Debra Yoder. The Village
     Health Worker in Review: An Annotated Bibliogra-
     phy. Public Administration Series, no. P-1341.
     Monticello, IL: Vance Bibliographies, 1982. 32p.
     Published and unpublished sources, primarily from
the 1970's and early 1980's, are arranged by author under
fourteen headings that include "Needs Assessment," "Community Organization," "Community and Institutional Support
Systems," etc.

301. De Benko, Eugene. "Rural Health in Africa: A Se-
     lected Bibliography," Rural Africana 17 (Winter
     1972):118-131.
     This bibliography "is intended to reflect the intri-
cacies facing rural health in Africa; it is based on the professional socio-medical literature of the last ten years with a
few relevant older citations. The bibliography is divided
into six groups: (1) African Folk Medicine and Traditional
Cures; (2) Child Care, Maternity, and Family Health; (3)
Nutrition and Food Problems; (4) Epidemics, Endemic Dis-
eases, and Other Disorders; (5) Mental Health; and (6) Rural Public Health and Modern Medical Services."
     The bibliography includes both French and English
language publications and is primarily devoted to journal
articles.

302. Fikry, Mona. Traditional Maternal and Child Care and
     Related Problems in the Sahel, A Bibliographic Study.
     Washington, D.C.: U.S. Agency for International
     Development, 1977. 123p.
     Pages 57 to 123 of this work comprise the annotated
bibliography. The more than 200 works listed concern both
medical and social aspects of maternal and child health care
in the Sahel. French and English languages are represented.

Monographs, journal articles, UN and government
documents from the 1960's and 1970's are emphasized. The
bibliography is arranged by author within several subject
sections. There is an author index.

303. Flax, James W., et al. Mental Health and Rural Amer-
     ica: An Overview and Annotated Bibliography.
     Rockville, MD: Division of Mental Health Service
     Programs, National Institute of Mental Health, 1979.
     viii + 216p. NTIS, SHR-0003706.
     The overview section of this work "places the men-
tal health problems and programs of rural areas in a broad
conceptual perspective." The bibliography section "is based
on an extensive review of the literature in medicine, psychia-
try, psychology, nursing, sociology, and social work. More
than 360 entries deal with a variety of conceptual and pro-
grammatic issues."
     The bibliography is divided into several chapters
and sub-chapters starting with the sociology of rural life and
continuing to rural social and psychological problems. While
the majority of the citations are to journal articles; books,
extension reports, government documents, and dissertations
and other unpublished papers are also included. Most works
cited date from the late 1960's through the middle 1970's.
Chapters or sub-chapters are arranged alphabetically by author. There is an author index.

304. Harrison, Elizabeth A. Emergency Medical Services:
     Rural Areas, 1964-Nov. 1980 (Citations from the
     NTIS Data Base). Springfield, VA: National
     Technical Information Service, 1980. 63p. PB81-
     800773.
     Unavailable for annotation.

305. Heald, Karen A., and James K. Cooper. An Annotated
     Bibliography on Rural Medical Care. Santa Monica,
     CA: Rand Corp., 1972. 39p. ED 078 149.
     "This bibliography lists and annotates books and
articles published since 1960 which are concerned with the
problems of rural health care and manpower. The bibliography is divided into three sections containing: (1) a subject
listing of the books and articles, including such areas as
manpower supply and distribution, need and demand for
health services, factors affecting physician placement, experience of programs to attract physicians, and alternative

approaches to the rural physician shortage, (2) an alphabetical listing of the references according to the author's name and including the title, publication information, and annotation, and (3) a table summarizing selected factors affecting physician location and factors related to rural living." The bibliography is not limited to the United States.

306. Jordan, Jeffrey L. Rural Health Care and International Development in Africa; With Additional Reference to Asia and Latin America. Exchange Bibliography, no. 1409. Monticello, IL: Council of Planning Librarians, 1977. 38p.

Works in this bibliography examine the relationship between population growth and improved health and the relationship between improved health and productivity. "The bibliographic materials presented here often concentrate on what has been called the integrated delivery of rural health care." The compiler defines this as "health programs that not only provide curative services, but also improved sanitation and water supplies, housing, family planning, nutrition and especially the provision of low-cost preventive medicine."

Most items selected for the bibliography were published since 1970 although a few earlier, standard sources are included. Statistical yearbooks and government reports presenting data but not discussing concepts are, for the most part, not included.

The bibliography is divided into ten sections: health and development, integrated delivery of rural health care, health and population, health planning, traditional medicine, maternal-child health, training of health personnel, the economics of disease, basic sources in health economics, and country studies. Books, articles, UN and U.S. government documents, dissertations, theses, and research and conference papers are included. There are no indexes.

307. Lee, Joel M., et al. Factors Influencing the Rural Location of Doctors and Students of Dentistry, Medicine, and Osteopathy. Exchange Bibliography, no. 1073. Monticello, IL: Council of Planning Librarians, 1976. 40p.

The compilers of this annotated bibliography identified works discussing factors in location decisions of doctors and students of medicine, dentistry, and osteopathy in the United States. From analyzing the works located, the

compilers noted 61 factors influencing location decisions.
The compilers state that the works listed in the bibliography
sometimes present conflicting interpretations of the influence
of these factors and also vary in the complexity of their interpretations. The 61 factors are listed at the beginning of
the bibliography. The works themselves each discuss from
one to 29 of the factors.
   Most of the works listed in this bibliography were
published in journals in the 1970's. Others were published
as reports, conference papers, or government documents.
Arrangement is by author. There are no indexes.

308. Mustian, R. David, et al. Rural Health Care: A Bib-
     liography. SRDC Bibliography Series, no. 10.
     Mississippi State: Southern Rural Development Cen-
     ter, 1980. 87p.
     "Specific foci of this bibliography are: 1. To as-
certain how community organization and structure influence
the delivery of health services.... 2. to determine how location of facilities and recruitment of personnel affect the
delivery of health services.... 3. to explore attitudes of
rural populations toward health and to determine if consen-
sus exists between health professionals and the general population concerning health needs."
   The bibliography aims to "systematically assemble
published works, project descriptions, and unpublished manuscripts." The period covered is 1965 to 1976. There is an
emphasis on the South as a region but literature concerning
other areas of the U.S. is sometimes included. There is an
author index and a subject index.

309. Physicians: Manpower Supply, Needs, and Demand,
     1964-1980 (Citations from the NTIS Data Base).
     Springfield, VA: National Technical Information
     Service, 1982. 290p. PB82-810375.
     Unavailable for annotation.

310. Physicians: Manpower Supply, Needs and Demand,
     1981-June 1982 (Citations from the NTIS Data Base).
     Springfield, VA: National Technical Information
     Service, 1982. 83p. PB82-810383.
     Unavailable for annotation.

311. Rural Health Services, December 1977-May 1983 (Cita-
     tions from the NTIS Data Base). Springfield, VA:

National Technical Information Service, 1983.   278p.
PB 83-806935.
Unavailable for annotation.

312.  SALUS:  Low-Cost Rural Health Care and Health Man-
      power Training:  An Annotated Bibliography with
      Special Emphasis on Developing Countries.   Ottawa:
      International Development Research Centre.   Vols.
      1-14.   1975-1984.
The International Development Research Centre has
established a computerized data base of information on rural
health care, emphasizing developing countries.   From this
data base they have issued 14 volumes of annotated bibliography during the period from 1975 through 1984.   (Note that
the first two volumes did not have "SALUS" at the beginning
of the titles.)   There are plans to publish a cumulative index
to these volumes.   Each volume contains approximately 700
entries arranged by author under subject headings and sub-
headings relating to organization and planning, implementation of health care, training and utilization of health workers,
and formal evaluative studies.   Each volume has subject, author, and geographic indexes.
      The Centre has made an effort to gather fugitive
literature for their data base and the bibliographies include a
variety of unpublished reports and papers as well as standard
sources such as journal articles, monographs, etc.   The bibliographies are not limited by date or language.

313.  Schofield, Sue.  Village Nutrition Studies:  An Anno-
      tated Bibliography.  [Brighton, U.K.]:  Village
      Studies Programme, Institute of Development Studies,
      University of Sussex, 1975.  xiii + 285p.
      This bibliography was produced as part of the ac-
tivities of the Village Studies Programme, Institute of Development Studies, University of Sussex.   It provides an extensive listing of both published and unpublished studies on
village nutrition requirements and concerns.
      Arrangement is by author within geographical region
and country.   "Each section is introduced by a short evalua-
tory comment on the surveys available, their quality and lim-
itations."   The citations are annotated, "indicating wherever
possible, the methods and results.   The annotation is followed
by the name(s) of the village(s) studied and where ascer-
tained, the district or region.   Most of the studies are available at the Institute of Development Studies (I.D.S.) but for

all studies listed in the main sections a location is included
at the bottom right hand corner of each entry." There are
no indexes.

314.   Sharma, Prakash C.   A Selected Research Bibliography
       on Planning and Delivery for Rural Health Services.
       Exchange Bibliography, no. 1313.   Monticello, IL:
       Council of Planning Librarians, 1977.   10p.
Items included in this bibliography were published
primarily between 1940 and 1975 and in addition to trade
publications include U.S. government documents, dissertations, conference papers, and commission reports.
The first section of the bibliography lists books
and monographs; the second articles and periodicals.   Within
each section entries are arranged alphabetically by author.
There are no indexes.

315.   Stahl, Sidney M., and Mary Suelmann.   Rural Physician
       Manpower: An Annotated Bibliography.   Studies in
       Health Care, Report No. 22.   Columbia:   Section of
       Health Care Studies, Dept. of Community Health and
       Medical Practice, School of Medicine, University of
       Missouri, 1971.   iii + 32p.
It is the authors' contention that multifactor research
needs to be undertaken on U.S. physician choice of location.
"The purpose of this annotated bibliography is to suggest the
scope of the variables that must be considered in a multifac-
torial design on the determination of physician location.   The
bibliography is divided into two sections.   Section I is concerned with studies that present data and general statements
about physician manpower today.   Section II deals with the
research that has employed the specific variables that influence the physician in determining his place of practice."
The variables considered include location of training facilities,
availability of medical facilities and related personnel, inter-
personal relations, etc.
       After the analyzed citations in Sections I and II, all
of the references are listed alphabetically by author.

316.   U.S. Dept. of Health, Education, and Welfare.   Public
       Health Service.   Division of Emergency Services.
       Rural Emergency Medical Services:   Selected Bibli-
       ography.   Washington, D.C.:   The Division, [1976?]
       iv + 24p.
       This extensively annotated bibliography lists govern-

ment documents and technical reports as well as articles from medical journals. All were published in the 1970's. "An effort has been made to cite material which is easily available and which documents new concepts and techniques, methodologies, innovations, and adaptations of local resources to EMS purposes." The bibliography ends with an author index.

# HOUSING

317. Burg, Nan C. Rural Poverty and Rural Housing: A
    Bibliography. Exchange Bibliography, no. 247.
    Monticello, IL: Council of Planning Librarians,
    1971. 23p.
        The bibliography is divided into five subject chap-
    ters: "Rural Housing--Books," "Rural Housing--Periodical
    References," "Rural Poverty--Books and Pamphlets," "Rural
    Poverty--Periodical References," and "Rural Housing and
    Rural Poverty--Continuing Reference Sources." All items
    deal with rural poverty and rural housing in the United
    States.
        Government documents are included in the "books
    and pamphlets" chapters. Entries are arranged by author
    within each chapter. Most entries date from 1960 through
    1971, although a few were published earlier in the century.
    There are no indexes.

318. Day, Savannah S. Housing Research Relevant to Rural
    Development: A Bibliography and Supplement.
    SRDC Rural Development Series, no. 5. Supple-
    ment 1. Mississippi State: Southern Rural Devel-
    opment Center, 1979. 150p.
        This work begins with a synthesis of research on
    rural housing published during 1970-1976 and is followed by
    an annotated bibliography divided into four sections: "Rural
    Housing Needs," "Design for Lower Cost Housing," "Remodel-
    ing/Rehabilitation," and "Home Financing." A wide range of
    works--journal articles, government documents, theses, dis-
    sertations, etc.--published between 1970 and 1976 is included.
    There is also an author index.
        Section II updates the bibliography through 1978
    and includes a listing of housing research projects in pro-
    gress or recently terminated.

319. Day, Savannah S., and Rosemary Carucci Goss. Research on Rural Housing: An Annotated Bibliography. Architecture Series, No. A-152. Monticello, IL: Vance Bibliographies, 1979. 45p.

"This bibliography primarily consists of research conducted at land grant colleges and universities, state agricultural experiment stations and government agencies." Arrangement is by author under ten topic divisions. Some of the topics--e.g., "Design and Construction"--relate to technical or economic aspects on rural housing. Others, such as "Housing Conditions and Needs," "Preferences and Satisfactions," etc., relate to sociological aspects. Most citations are to works written in the 1970's. All concern housing issues in the United States.

# IRRIGATION

320. Ellingson, Dennis, and K. William Easter. A Review
    and an Annotated Bibliography of Studies Regard-
    ing Irrigation Institutions, Management and Invest-
    ment in Asia. [St. Paul, MN]: Dept. of Agricul-
    tural and Applied Economics, [University of Minne-
    sota], 1982. 49p.
    The annotated bibliography, which constitutes ap-
proximately half of this document, emphasizes journal articles and research papers. Both sociological and economic
literature is included. With one exception works included
were published between 1970 and 1981. Annotations are extensive and arrangement is alphabetical by author. There
are no indexes.

321. Gellar, Sheldon. Planning, Management and Participa-
    tory Development Issues in Irrigation Projects: A
    Select Annotated Bibliography. [Ougadougou, Up-
    per Volta]: Permanent Interstate Committee for
    Drought Control in the Sahel/CILSS; [Paris]: Or-
    ganization for Economic Cooperation and Develop-
    ment, 1981. i + 64 leaves.
    "Most of the literature covered in this paper has
been written by social scientists and irrigation specialists
who have worked in the field, and deals with the human
and organizational factors often neglected by irrigation
planners." Almost all entries are in English and were published between 1970 and 1981. Entries include lengthy annotations of books and parts of books, periodical articles,
unpublished papers, government and UN documents, dissertations, theses, and research reports.
    The bibliography is multidisciplinary, comparative
(i.e., does not limit itself to literature on the Sahel) and
multidimensional in perspective (i.e., reflects concerns of
local populations as well as managers and planners).

The bibliography is organized into several subject
chapters: "Planning and Management," "Political, Social,
and Economic Impact of Irrigation Projects," "Sahelian West
Africa," "Case Studies," and "Resource Guide to Irrigation."
The last category includes other bibliographies, journals,
and a listing of irrigation research institutes and networks.
Within chapters or sub-chapters the bibliography is
arranged by author. There is an index by author and by
geography.

322. International Rice Research Institute and Agricultural
     Development Council. Bibliography on Socio-
     economic Aspects of Irrigation in Asia. Singapore:
     The Institute, 1976. 80p.
     Journal articles and technical reports, as well as
theses, dissertations, and published and unpublished research papers, are the focus of this bibliography. The
bibliography is organized into several subject chapters on
specific economic and social aspects of irrigation projects.
The compilers state that "emphasis was given to research
literature having operational implications, either to the for-
mulation of irrigation policy or to the planning, design, and
management of irrigation systems. The bibliography is
therefore intended to cover applied research which could
influence decisions in irrigation development."
     While the bibliography emphasizes "gravity flow
canals in the humid tropics" of Asia, some research in other
systems and locations was included. Most items in the bibliography were published in the 1960's and early 1970's although some earlier works are included.
     There is an appendix providing a list of abbrevia-
tions used in this bibliography and one providing an index
by country.

323. Jones, E.A. Irrigation and Human Adaptation.
     Commonwealth Bureau of Agricultural Economics.
     Annotated Bibliography, no. 19. Commonwealth
     Agricultural Bureaux, 1973. ii + 8p.
     The citations and annotations in this bibliography
were selected from World Agricultural Economics and Rural
Sociology Abstracts, 1971-1973. Arrangement is by author
under geographical region.

324. Jones, Garth N., et al. Informational Sources on
     Water Management for Agricultural Production in

Pakistan with Special Reference to Institutional and
Human Factors. Water Management Technical Report, no. 31. Fort Collins: Colorado State University, 1974. Vol. I, xii + 170p.; Vol. II, iv +
251p.
Volume II of this report consists of a comprehensive, partially annotated bibliography on agricultural water
management in Pakistan. Arrangement is by author within a
detailed subject outline. There is a concluding author index.

325. Lehmann, E.J. Public Opinion and Sociology of Water
Resource Development: A Bibliography with Abstracts. Springfield, VA: National Technical Information Service, 1977. PS-77/0432.
Unavailable for annotation.

LABOR / INDUSTRY

326. Annotated Bibliography on Migrant Farmworkers Issues.
      Rosslyn, VA: Interamerica Research Associates,
      1979.
      Unavailable for annotation.

327. Armstrong, Douglas, and Kristeen Krestensen. Agri-
      cultural Labour in Canada and United States: A
      Bibliography. [Toronto]: Research Library, On-
      tario Ministry of Labour, 1973. 40 leaves.
      The first 5½ leaves of this bibliography are devoted
      to agricultural labor in Canada; the rest to agricultural labor
      in the United States. Monographs; periodical articles; and
      U.S., Canadian, state, provincial, and UN documents are
      listed by author within each section. Almost all entries date
      from the 1960's through the early 1970's. Asterisks indicate
      those items owned by the Ontario Ministry of Labour. There
      are no indexes.

328. Condon, E.C. Bibliography on Migrants and Migrant
      Education, 1981-1982. Series A, Reference Materi-
      als. New Brunswick, NJ: Institute for Intercul-
      tural Relations and Ethnic Studies, Rutgers, The
      State University, 1982. 47p. ED 238 598.
      The 379 entries in this bibliography were mostly
      published between 1970 and 1980 and come from the collec-
      tion of the Rutgers Intercultural and Ethnic Studies Institute.
      Arrangement is by author within subject headings that in-
      clude family, health, labor, housing, programs, etc. Ap-
      pendices list relevant federal and state agencies and addi-
      tional sources of information.

329. Connell, John. Labour Utilization: An Annotated
      Bibliography of Village Studies. [Brighton, U.K.]:
      Village Studies Programme, Institute of Development
      Studies, University of Sussex, 1975. xv + 305p.

"This bibliography complements a Village Studies
Programme (VSP) report on village labour situations sub-
mitted to the International Labour Organization in 1973, and
attempts to list and summarize all village surveys from the
Third World that are oriented to labour utilization, include
information on labour utilization, and/or have particular sorts
of related information.... The bibliography aims to be as
comprehensive as possible for studies carried out between
1950 and 1973...."
     Arrangement is alphabetical by author within geo-
graphical region and country. Entries are annotated and are
coded from 25 categories relating to occupational structure,
labor inputs, wages/productivity, etc. Each of these category numbers also reveals whether the category information
is for the aggregate population or a sub-group thereof. The
presence in the study of quantitative data, qualitative data,
or no data is also indicated for each entry. There are no
indexes.

330. Crow, Susan B., and Arneada Bray Russell. Selected
     Technical Assistance Resource Agencies and an An-
     notated Bibliography for Rural Employment and
     Training Practitioners in Virginia. Richmond:
     Center for Public Affairs, Virginia Commonwealth
     University, 1983. 71p. ED 241 219.
     The first half of this work summarizes interviews
with representatives from nonprofit organizations that provide technical assistance to rural employment and training
practitioners in Virginia. The second half is an annotated
list of relevant books, reports, newsletters, etc. All citations are to works published since 1975.

331. Haque, Serajul. A Select Bibliography on Agricultural/
     Rural Labour (Employment, unemployment & under-
     employment). BIDS Library Documentation Series.
     BIDS Library Bibliography Series, no. 4. Dacca:
     Bangladesh Institute of Development Studies, 1976.
     18p.
     While not restricted by type or date of publication,
most entries in this brief bibliography are journal articles
published in the 1960's or 1970's. The bibliography is not
limited by geographical region. Arrangement is alphabetical
by author. There are no indexes.

332. Jessee, D.L., and R.H. Brannon. Unemployment and

Underemployment in Rural Sectors of the Less Developed Countries: A Bibliography. Occasional
Paper, no. 6. [Washington, D.C.]: Economics and
Sector Planning Division, Technical Assistance Bureau, U.S. Agency for International Development,
1977. v + 148p.
"This bibliography results from a literature search
done for the preparation of papers for U.S.A.I.D. and
U.S.D.A. which dealt with rural sector unemployment and
underemployment in less developed countries. Four major
subject areas are treated: the nature and scope of employment and income problems; technological impacts upon employment and income; agrarian sector policies designed to
increase employment and income; and general discussions of
the roles of the rural sector and other sectors in regional
or national economic development. These four areas are
further divided into thirteen topical areas arranged by geography. The literature, all written within the last 20 years,
is limited mainly to English language publications and to a
selected number of journals, books, and publications of major
international organizations. Documents which are not specific
to a region and which have useful information are organized
into sections titled 'In General' at the beginning of each topic.
Some works are cross listed among topics. The emphasis in
this collection of over 1400 works is upon those materials
which provide economic analyses and interpretations."

333.    Kale, Stephen. The Impact of New or Additional In-
        dustry upon Rurally Oriented Areas: A Selectively
        Annotated Bibliography with Emphasis on Manufactur-
        ing. Exchange Bibliography, no. 1148. Monticello,
        IL: Council of Planning Librarians, 1976. 28p.
        Originally published as University of Nebraska-
Lincoln Bureau of Business Research Occasional Paper No. 2
in March 1973, this bibliography contains a partially annotated listing by author of studies of the effects of industry on
rural areas. "For the most part these studies have been
conducted by the various state agricultural experiment stations or by bureaus of business and economic research.
Some theses and dissertations have also been undertaken...."
Date of publication of the studies is from the early 1950's
through early 1970's. All concern rural areas of the United
States.

334.    Kjaer-Olsen, Pia. A Preliminary Bibliography on Rural

Employment in Botswana. Gaborone: Republic of
Botswana, 1979. 25 leaves.
"The following preliminary bibliography is an attempt to gather together the many published and unpublished studies, surveys, reports and articles which deal
with any aspect of rural employment in Botswana. 'Rural
employment' is understood in its broadest sense to cover
any form of gaining a livelihood such as hunting and gathering, subsistence farming, cash cropping, wage labor, rural
entrepreneurship and village industries."
Most citations are to works from the 1970's. The
bibliography is arranged in one list, alphabetically by author.
There are no indexes.

335.  Krannich, Richard S., and John F. Schnell.  Social
      and Economic Impacts of U.S. Industrial Develop-
      ment:  A Working Bibliography.  Exchange Bibli-
      ography, no. 1365.  Monticello, IL:  Council of
      Planning Librarians, 1977.  12p.
      This is a selected bibliography of a wide range of
literature.  The compilers intend to "provide at least an initial listing of literature which most directly addresses the
major issues of rural industrial development in the U.S."
Arrangement is by author and is not limited by date of publication.

336.  Little, Ronald L., and Stephen B. Lovejoy.  Western
      Energy Development as a Type of Rural Industriali-
      zation:  A Partially Annotated Bibliography.  Ex-
      change Bibliography, no. 1298.  Monticello, IL:
      Council of Planning Librarians, 1977.  39p.
      Specific subjects covered in this bibliography in-
clude "(1) rural industrialization, (2) rural energy development, (3) rural employment patterns, (4) attitudes toward
energy development, (5) rural household economics and family structure, (6) demographic characteristics of national and
regional populations, (7) demographic characteristics of energy
project construction workers, (8) impacts of energy developments in the Rocky Mountains and Northern Great Plains,
(9) environmental impact assessment, (10) proposed and completed energy developments in the U.S., (11) Indian reservation politics, (12) Indian reservation political structure,
(13) Indian reservation economic structures (family and tri-
bal), and (14) Indian attitudes toward energy development."
      In the introduction the authors note that much of

the literature relevant to the subject is difficult to locate
through standard sources. The authors succeeded in identifying books and book reviews, articles, government documents, conference papers, theses and other unpublished research papers, and newspaper articles. The majority of the
items included were published in the 1960's or 1970's, although some date from earlier decades. Most entries are
annotated, some at length. The arrangement is alphabetical
by author. There are no indexes.

337.  Meyer, Richard L., and Adelaida Alicbusan. Annotated
      Bibliography on Rural Off-Farm Employment. Vol. I.
      Economics and Sociology Occasional Paper, no. 659.
      Columbus: Agricultural Finance Program, Dept. of
      Agricultural Economics and Rural Sociology, Ohio
      State University, 1979. ii + 65 leaves.
      Journal articles, dissertations and other unpublished
research papers, and government and UN reports, mostly
dating from the 1970's, are listed by author. The bibliography "focuses on the results of long-term research and large-
ly ignores the substantial number of consultant reports and
project documents available which deal with specific projects
and programs. The emphasis is on research conducted in
LDC's, but many other items of general methodological and
theoretical interest are also included." Arrangement is by
author. There are no indexes.

338.  Meyer, Richard L., and Harpal S. Grewal. Annotated
      Bibliography on Rural Off-Farm Employment. Vol.
      II. Economics and Sociology Occasional Paper, no.
      1016. Columbus: Agricultural Finance Program,
      Dept. of Agricultural Economics and Rural Sociology,
      Ohio State University, 1983. 83p.
      Volume II of this title emphasizes publications that
became available to the compilers after the first volume was
published in 1979. It concludes with an author and a geographic index.

339.  Migrant Workers, 1964-October 1981 (Citations from the
      NTIS Data Base). Springfield, VA: National Tech-
      nical Information Service, 1981. 110p. NTIS, PB82-
      801283.
      Unavailable for annotation.

340.  Renton, Margaret Ann. The Migratory Farm Labor

Problem: A Select Bibliography. Government Publications Bibliography, no. 10. Irvine: Government
Publications Dept., University Library, University
of California, 1975. 32 leaves.
This bibliography is a compilation of U.S. and California government documents located in the University of
California, Irvine Library and relating to migratory farm
labor. There is no restriction by date of publication.
The bibliography is organized into several subject
chapters--e.g., education, employment, and housing--some
of which have sub-chapters. Within chapters or sub-
chapters entries are arranged by authoring agency or department. There are no indexes.

341. Ruesink, David C., and Karen Nergart. Bibliography
     Relating to Contemporary American Agricultural
     Labor: A Supplement to the Bibliography Relating
     to Agricultural Labor. Departmental Information
     Report 73-4. College Station: Texas Agricultural
     Experiment Station, Dept. of Agricultural Economics
     and Rural Sociology, Texas A & M University, 1973.
     This bibliography, intended to supplement a 1969
publication, Bibliography Relating to Agricultural Labor, and
also published as a Departmental Information Report, includes
economic as well as sociological literature. It is organized by
type of material--"Published Bibliographies," "Books," "Dissertations," "Proceedings," "Bulletins," "U.S. Government
Documents," and "Periodicals." Within these chapters arrangement is by author. There is some attempt at subject
indexing by providing one or more established category
terms after each citation. A "Cross Reference" list also
provides indexing under 24 broad terms.

342. Selvik, Arne, and Gene F. Summers. Social Impacts
     of Nonmetro Industrial Growth: Annotated Bibliog-
     raphy of U.S. Case Studies. SRDC Series Publica-
     tion, no. 18. Mississippi State: Southern Rural
     Development Center, 1977. 55p. + vii. ED 156 405.
     "The bibliography presents annotations of a number
of articles from journals within the discipline of social science, the names and publishers of which appear in the appendix. The articles, most of them written by economists,
geographers, and sociologists, cover the period from 1965
to 1974. In addition, a large number of research reports
(Master's and Ph.D. dissertations, Experiment Station Bulletins and so on) have been annotated."

Items selected are concerned with empirical assessment of rural community response to a manufacturing site built since 1945.

Arrangement is alphabetical by author. There are no indexes. The bibliography "can be seen as supplementary to and as a systematic extension of a bibliography by Gene F. Summers and his associates."

343.  Smith, Eldon D., et al. Industrialization of Rural Areas: A Bibliography. Rural Development Bibliography Series, no. 1. SRDC Bibliography Series, no. 1. Mississippi State: Southern Rural Development Center, [1977?] 155p.

"The more than 750 entries, many annotated, cover available research, extension, and action agency literature released mainly from 1960-76." Arrangement is alphabetical by author. The bibliography is preceded by a classification system which has two sections. One is oriented to nontechnical users and the other to technical and professional users.

344.  Summers, Gene F.; Sharon Evans; and Jon Minkoff. Rural Industrial Development Bibliography: Selected Impact Study Documents. Working Paper RID 75.1. Madison: Center of Applied Sociology, University of Wisconsin, 1975. 23p. ED 135 571.

The 186 documents in this bibliography reflect social science research on "the measurable impact of new industry on demographic, economic and/or social dimensions of rural community life in the U.S. Restricting the meaning of 'industrial development' to the location of new manufacturing plants, this bibliography includes documents which report data from an empirical assessment of a new plant site having occurred between 1945 and 1975 and having had measured impacts." Some citations are to works from the 1950's, most are from the 1960's and 1970's. The compilers note their efforts in gathering fugitive literature as well as that located through standard bibliographic sources.

345.  Velji, Shirin. Bibliography: Labor and Employment and Related Topics, 1970-1975. Employment and Rural Development Division, Development Economics Dept., International Bank for Reconstruction and Development [IBRD], 1975.

While some works concerning urban areas are included in this bibliography the emphasis is on works dealing with rural labor and employment. A wide range of journal articles, books, research papers, government documents, etc. is included. Arrangement is alphabetical by author with no subject divisions or indexes.

346. Balasubramanian, Krishnamurthy. Bibliography on
     Agrarian Tensions and Land Reforms. New Delhi:
     Documentation Centre, Gandhi Peace Foundation
     [1972?], 33 + 68 leaves.
     This bibliography on Indian publications is organ-
ized into a section on agrarian unrest and one on land reforms. Within each section books, journal articles, newspaper articles, and reports and seminars are listed separately.
The emphasis in the bibliography is on the 1970-1972 period.
All newspaper entries date from this period; coverage of
journals and books includes earlier material. The bibliography concludes with author, subject, and title indexes and a
list of journals and newspapers surveyed.

347. Baron, Donald. Land Reform in Sub-Saharan Africa:
     An Annotated Bibliography. [Washington, D.C.]:
     [U.S.] Agency for International Development, under
     RSSA USDA 4.77, 1978. 46 leaves. Draft.
     "The purpose of this annotated bibliography is to
summarize the views presented in recent books and articles
that have studied the relationship between land tenure and
economic development in Sub-Saharan Africa. This summary
is divided into five annotation sections, each of which review
[sic] a specific land reform issue or set of related issues.
The bibliography section accompanying each annotation then
lists the books and articles which present in-depth analyses
of those issues. A number of publications which discuss
several issues are therefore cited in more than one bibliography section."
     The five issues into which the bibliography is di-
vided are: "The Group-Ownership Pattern," "The Individualization Process," "New Land Tenure Problems Created by
the Individualization Process," "Land Registration and Consolidation: Possible Solutions to the Problems of Uncertainty

and Fragmentation," and "Land Reform in Kenya." Approximately 30 items appear in each of the five bibliographies. There are no indexes.

348. Commonwealth Bureau of Agricultural Economics. Land and Population in Agricultural Development. Annotated Bibliography, no. 33. Commonwealth Agricultural Bureaux, 1974. 24p.

"The selection of 150 references has been made from abstracts published in World Agricultural Economics and Rural Sociology Abstracts (WAERSA) between 1964 and August 1974." The subject of land and population in relation to agricultural development is broadly defined to include descriptions of land tenure systems as well as some migration and settlement studies.

"The bibliography begins with general and theoretical studies, followed by references on developing countries, sub-divided by region and further by country." There are no indexes.

349. Commonwealth Bureau of Agricultural Economics. The Role of Private Plots in Socialist Agriculture. Annotated Bibliography, no. 7. Commonwealth Agricultural Bureaux, 1971. iii + 9p.

Compiled from World Agricultural Economics and Rural Sociology Abstracts, the bibliography is arranged, after a general section, by country and author. Works included were published between the mid-1960's and 1970.

350. Commonwealth Bureau of Agricultural Economics. Tourism and Recreation in Rural Areas: Aspects of Land Use Planning and Structural Change (1965-1971). Edited by K.P. Broadbent. Annotated Bibliography, no. 11. Commonwealth Agricultural Bureaux, 1972. 16p. Supplement, 1974. 11p.

"This bibliography contains abstracts of articles, which have previously appeared in World Agricultural Economics and Rural Sociology Abstracts (WAERSA) during the period 1965-1971, dealing with rural aspects of the tourist industry. They are classified first geographically and then alphabetically by author. A supplementary list of title references is appended for publications held jointly by the Bureau and the Institute of Agricultural Economics.... These titles have not been previously abstracted in WAERSA." The bibliography concludes with a subject index.

351.  Cyprus Bibliography on Land Tenure and Settlement.
      Nicosia, Cyprus:  Land Consolidation Authority,
      1972.  5 leaves.
      This brief bibliography includes both English and
Greek language publications without restriction as to date of
publication.  Section A lists "Books and Reprints," Section
B, "Papers."  Within sections arrangement is alphabetical by
author.

352.  Davis, Lenwood G.  Land Usage, Reforms and Planning
      in Africa:  An Introductory Survey.  Exchange Bib-
      liography, no. 1372.  Monticello, IL:  Council of
      Planning Librarians, 1977.  13p.
      Organized by type of material--articles, books, and
dissertations and theses--this bibliography includes works
published as early as 1927, although most date from the
1960's and 1970's.  Within each section the arrangement is
alphabetical by author.  There are no indexes.

353.  Developing Countries:  Land Use and Irrigation.  Jan-
      uary 1971-May 1971 (Citations from the NTIS Data
      Base).  NTIS, PB 81-864837.
      Unavailable for annotation.

354.  Eckert, Jerry.  Lesotho's Land Tenure:  An Análysis
      and Annotated Bibliography.  Lesotho Agricultural
      Sector Analysis Project.  Special Bibliography, no.
      2.  Fort Collins:  Economics Dept., Colorado State
      University, 1980.  45p + 9p.
      Introductory sections present an overview of the
history of land law in Lesotho and a discussion of land tenure issues.  The annotated bibliography attempts to be comprehensive in its listing of "the world's literature containing
original substance regarding Lesotho's land tenure."

355.  Food and Agriculture Organization of the United Na-
      tions.  Bibliography on Land Settlement.  Rome:
      FAO, 1976.  viii + 146p.
      Monographs and articles published between 1958 and
1975 are included in this bibliography.  Several languages
are represented.
      "In the context of the bibliography, land settlement
is conceived as the planned movement of populations to areas
of under-utilized agricultural potential.  The Bibliography
also contains references on projects for the settlement of

nomads, refugees, youth, pensioners, and for persons dis-
placed by the construction of dams and by natural disaster,
as well as literature on settlement policy, land administration,
land consolidation, village modernization and the improvement
of rural infrastructure. It encompasses development of both
rainfed and irrigated agriculture and includes various types
of farms, ranging from state farms through collective and cooperative farms to individual smallholdings."

The bibliography begins with a general chapter and
is then organized by geographical regions. There is a general listing at the beginning of each regional division and
then a listing by country. Within each section entries are
arranged by author. There is an author index and a list of
periodicals indexed.

356.  Food and Agriculture Organization of the United Na-
      tions. Bibliography on Land Tenure. Rome:  Rural
      Institutions Division, FAO, 1972.  374p.

      Designed to provide "information on monographs and
articles on land tenure systems and agrarian reform programmes," this bibliography includes a wide variety of works
in several languages. It is organized by continent and country and then alphabetically by author. An earlier volume
was published in 1955 and a supplement in 1959. This volume covers the 1958-1970 publication period. There is an
author index.

357.  Food and Agriculture Organization of the United Na-
      tions. Land Reform:  Annotated Bibliography; FAO
      Publications and Documents (1945-April 1970).
      [Rome?]:  Documentation Centre, FAO, 1971.

      This computer-generated bibliography covers works
on land reform and related subjects. The annotations consist of an "indexing synopsis" in which the subject of the
document is described in one or more sentences containing
several descriptors which are then used as access points in
the analytical index.

      Each entry has an identification number which in-
cludes FAO accession number, year of publication, and document type as well as country or region that is the subject
of the document, language(s) in which it is available, and
other information on the document's origin and availability.

      Arrangement is by accession number. There is an
author index as well as the extensive analytical index.

358. Hammons, V. Alvin. "Land Use: A Select Bibliography," Rural Africana 23 (Winter 1974):91-96.
Items in this bibliography relate to land use in Africa and "were selected primarily for their methodological approach." Some unpublished research papers are included but the emphasis is on books and journal articles without restriction by date of publication. Arrangement is alphabetical by author.

359. Harvey, Prentice. The Social and Economic Consequences of Industry in Small Communities and Rural Areas: An Annotated Bibliography. Exchange Bibliography, no. 940. Monticello, IL: Council of Planning Librarians, 1975. 17p.
Items listed in this bibliography are those concerned only with the social and economic and not the environmental consequences of industry in small communities and rural areas. With a few exceptions, works included deal only with rural areas of the United States.
The bibliography is organized by type of material: books, monographs, and dissertations; articles and bulletins; reports and occasional papers. Within these divisions entries are arranged by author. Some entries have brief annotations; all were published between 1939 and 1974. There are no indexes.

360. Ijere, M.O. Source Materials for the Study of African Land Tenure. Departmental Research Notes, no. 2. Nsukka: Dept. of Agricultural Management, University of Nigeria, 1974. 18 leaves.
Journal articles, monographs, government documents, and published and unpublished papers, without restriction by date, are listed by author. There are no indexes.

361. Karouzis, G., and P. Ioannides. Bibliography on Land Tenure in Cyprus. Nicosia, Cyprus: Land Consolidation Authority, 1974. 26 leaves.
This is an expanded version of Cyprus Bibliography on Land Tenure and Settlement published by the Land Consolidation Authority in 1972. The arrangement is by author within sections on "Books and Reprints," "Papers," and "Legislation." Both Greek and English language publications are included without restriction by date of publication.

362. Land in Micronesia and Its Resources: An Annotated

Bibliography. Compiled by E.H. Bryan and staff
for the Trust Territory of the Pacific Islands.
Honolulu, Hawaii: Pacific Scientific Information
Center, Bernice P. Bishop Museum, 1970. 119p.
All aspects of land resources, use, tenure, and classification in Micronesia are covered in this bibliography.
Entries are arranged in one alphabetical list by author and
are not restricted either by date of publication or type of
material--i.e., books, periodical articles, government documents, theses, etc. are included. Much of this bibliography
is historical in nature and some of it refers to biological and
geological rather than social research. Several languages are
represented in the bibliography. The bibliography concludes
with an "Index to Subjects and Areas."

363. Land Reform: A Selected List of References for A.I.D.
     Technicians. A.I.D. Bibliography Series: Agricul-
     ture, no. 4. Washington, D.C.: Office of Agricul-
     ture and Fisheries, Bureau for Technical Assistance
     in cooperation with A.I.D. Reference Center, 1970.
     v + 51p.
     The focus of this annotated bibliography is A.I.D.
reports and documents, especially publications of the Land
Tenure Center at the University of Wisconsin. Other studies,
including dissertations, are also included. The majority of
works listed were published in the 1960's, the rest in the
1950's.
     The first part of the bibliography is arranged by
subject. The following sections are arranged by region and
country. Concluding sections list bibliographies, unannotated materials, doctoral dissertations, additional material, and
A.I.D. Spring Review Materials. There are no indexes.

364. Long, Burl F. A Bibliography: Land Use Issues.
     SRDC Bibliography Series, no. 9. Mississippi State:
     Southern Rural Development Center, 1981.
     Unavailable for annotation.

365. Mather, A.S., and R.J. Ardern. An Annotated Bibli-
     ography of Rural Land Use in the Highlands and
     Islands of Scotland. O'Dell Memorial Monograph,
     no. 9. Aberdeen: Dept. of Geography, University
     of Aberdeen, 1981. 193p.
     While much of this bibliography is unrelated to con-
temporary rural sociology, it does include some significant

citations. Relevant subject chapters are "General," "Policies, Legislation and Planning," "Land Ownership, Tenure and Organization," and "Crofting." Even within these chapters much of the information is historical in nature. A wide variety of published and unpublished literature is included. Within each subject chapter items are arranged by geographical and sub-region and historical period. The bibliography concludes with "Bibliographies and bibliographical sources"; a "List of relevant acts, bills, and papers"; a "Sub-regional index"; a "Place name index"; an "Author index"; and a "Historical index."

366. Meliczek, Hans. Bibliography on Land Tenure and Related Subjects in St. Lucia and Other Caribbean Territories. Castries, St. Lucia, West Indies: Ministry of Trade, Industry, Agriculture and Tourism, 1973. 12 leaves.
    This bibliography is organized into sections on "Monographs and articles referring to the West Indies including St. Lucia," "Monographs and articles referring to individual territories in the West Indies," and "Legislative provisions of St. Lucia." Meliczek was the FAO Land Tenure Advisor in St. Lucia when he compiled the bibliography.

367. Mesfin Kinfu. Bibliography on Land Tenure, Land Reform and Rural Land Use in Ethiopia. [Addis Ababa?]: Ministry of Land Reform and Administration.
    Unavailable for annotation.

368. New York [State] Agricultural Resources Commission. A Selected, Annotated Bibliography on Agricultural Land Use in New York State. Prepared by J.P. Sullivan. Albany, NY: The Commission, 1976. vi + 24 leaves.
    While some monographs and journal articles are included in this bibliography, the majority of citations are to state and federal documents, commission reports, and extension papers published by Cornell University. Most entries have a publication date ranging from the mid-1960's to 1976. While most entries deal exclusively with New York State, some are broader in scope but relevant to the state.
    The bibliography is organized into five subject chapters: "Urbanization and Agriculture," "Land Use Legislation and Policy," "Geographical Patterns," "Economic Aspects," and "Land Use Classification/Inventory." Within

chapters entries are arranged alphabetically by author.
There are no indexes.

369. Ofori, Patrick E.  Land in Africa: Its Administration,
     Law, Tenure and Use; A Select Bibliography.
     Nendeln [Liechtenstein]:  KTO Press, 1978.  vii +
     200p.

"The bibliography attempts to list books, articles,
memoranda, theses, legislation and other relevant material
dealing with all aspects of land in Africa.  It includes material on such complex and controversial topics as customary
land law and tenure, land use, ownership and property
rights, security of tenure, land administration, settlement
patterns, urban land problems, land registration, cadastral
surveys, land policies, land reform, resettlement, irrigation,
land valuation, and land taxation."
     The bibliography is organized by regions within
Africa and then by country.  Under individual countries,
entries are arranged alphabetically by author.  There are
author and subject indexes and an appendix listing publications of the Land Administration Research Centre, University of Science and Technology, Kumasi, Ghana.

370. Ramakrishnan, S.  Land Reform in Developing Coun-
     tries:  Select Bibliography on Land Reform (1973-
     1977).  Lincoln Institute Monograph, no. 78-5.
     Cambridge, MA:  Lincoln Institute of Land Policy,
     1978.  v + 63p.

"This compilation covers books, journal articles,
seminar and conference papers and reports on the subjects
of land reform, land tenure and land policies in developing
countries published or written during the last five years,
1973-1977."
     The bibliography is organized into five sections.
The general section lists materials not limited by geographical region.  The remaining sections are on Africa, Asia and
the Far East, Latin America and Oceania, and the Middle
East.  Within each section arrangement is first by year and
then by author.  There are no indexes.

371. University of Wisconsin.  Land Tenure Center Library.
     Agrarian Reform in Latin America:  An Annotated
     Bibliography.  Madison:  Land Tenure Center
     Library, 1974.  xvi + 667p.
     This is a complete listing of relevant holdings in

the University of Wisconsin-Madison Libraries as of October
1973. Location information is provided for each item.

The bibliography is organized into three geographical regions--Latin America, Central America, and the Caribbean. Within each there is a general section and then a division by country. There are personal author, corporate
author, and classified subject indexes.

372. University of Wisconsin. Land Tenure Center Library.
Land Tenure and Agrarian Reform in Africa and the
Near East: An Annotated Bibliography. Compiled
by the staff of the Land Tenure Center Library
under the direction of Teresa J. Anderson. Boston,
MA: G.K. Hall, 1976. xxiv + 423p.

This bibliography includes only titles that are available in one of the libraries of the University of Wisconsin-
Madison. Each entry indicates in which library the title can
be found. Books, reports, articles, and pamphlets are included.

All African nations and territories are included except the Cape Verde Islands, Comoro Islands, Equatorial
Guinea, French Territory of the Afars and Issas, Guinea-
Bissau, Namibia, São Tomé and Príncipe, Spanish Sahara,
and Seychelles. Within the section on the "Arabian Peninsula," only Saudi Arabia is listed individually. Exclusions
result from the lack of substantive information.

After an initial section on Africa in general, the
book is organized by name of country with entries arranged
by author. There is a personal author index, a corporate
author index, and a subject index. The subject index is
preceded by a classified outline.

373. University of Wisconsin. Land Tenure Center Library.
Land Tenure and Agrarian Reform in East and Southeast Asia: An Annotated Bibliography. Compiled
by the staff of the Land Tenure Center Library
under the direction of Teresa J. Anderson. Boston,
MA: G.K. Hall, 1980. xxviii + 557p.

This bibliography includes books, articles, reports
and pamphlets that are available in one of the libraries of
the University of Wisconsin-Madison. Entries indicate which
library owns them.

The initial section on land reform in general is followed by a section on land reform in Asia. The remainder
of the book is organized by country with entries arranged

by author's name.  All Asian countries except for Pacific
Islands are included.  There is a personal name index, a
corporate name index, and a subject index.  A classified
outline of the subject index precedes it.

374.  University of Wisconsin.  Land Tenure Center Library.
      Colonization and Settlement:  A Bibliography.
      Training & Methods Series, no. 8.  Madison:  Land
      Tenure Center Library, 1969.  41p.  Supplement,
      1971, 21p.
      Holdings of the Land Tenure Center Library re-
lated to agricultural colonization are listed without restriction by date, type of publication, or language.  After an
introductory general section the bibliography is arranged by
country and then by author.  In the bibliography, in contrast to the supplement, there is also a division between
books and pamphlets, periodical articles, and microfilm.
There are no indexes.  A call number or other information
necessary for locating the item in the Land Tenure Center
Library is found next to each entry.

375.  West, H.W., and O.H.M. Sawyer.  Land Administra-
      tion:  A Bibliography for Developing Countries.
      Cambridge, U.K.  Dept. of Land Economy, Cam-
      bridge University, 1975.  x + 292p.
      Conference papers and proceedings, books, and
journal articles on land ownership, tenure and law, and land
policy and administration are listed in this bibliography.
Items included were published between 1963 and 1975 and
deal specifically with a developing country or region rather
than with general principles or theories.
      After an initial general section, entries are ar-
ranged by continent and country.  Within each section entries are arranged alphabetically by author.  There is an
author index and an index of countries.

376. Connell, John. Rural Migration in Less Developed
     Countries: A Preliminary Bibliography. Occasional
     Guides, no. 3. Brighton [U.K.]: Library, Insti-
     tute of Development Studies, University of Sussex,
     [1973?]. vi + 62p.
     As the title indicates, this bibliography is limited,
with few exceptions, to rural migration in less developed
countries. Additionally, "in most cases ... work on international migration is excluded, as are statistical studies of
internal migrations which provide little information on the
causes of migration. The bias is towards socio-economic
accounts of migration, rather than genetic or psychological
aspects and some special classes of population are not referred to, e.g., commuters, pilgrims, nomads. Most of the
references, all dating from post-1950, deal with permanent,
semi-permanent or seasonal migrations and the range of possible 'push' factors in such movements."
     The bibliography was compiled in conjunction with
the Village Studies Project at the Institute of Development
Studies and contains approximately 500 references up to the
end of 1972. It is arranged into sections on Africa, Asia,
Latin America, and the West Indies, under which there is
further grouping by country and by author. There are no
indexes.

377. Gober, Patricia. An Annotated Bibliography of Popu-
     lation Growth and Migration of Nonmetropolitan
     Areas of the U.S. Public Administration Series,
     no. P-419. Monticello, IL: Vance Bibliographies,
     1980. 31p.
     The 1970 U.S. census showed that the historical
trend of migration from rural into urban areas had been
reversed. This bibliography "is a reflection of the state
of the arts in the area of nonmetropolitan population growth

and migration. The material is primarily descriptive in nature although there have been some attempts to identify processes that underlie changing population distribution."
Books, journal articles, government documents, dissertations and other unpublished research papers are arranged in one alphabetical list by author.

378.  Haque, Serajul, and Shamsul Islam Khan. Spatial Distribution: Rural and Urban; A Select Bibliography. BIDS Library Documentation Series. BIDS Library Bibliography Series, no. 7. Dacca: Bangladesh Institute of Development Studies, 1976. 11p.
     This brief bibliography primarily lists periodical articles and conference proceedings from the 1960's and early 1970's. Many entries concern internal rural-urban migration. The bibliography is not limited by geography. It is arranged alphabetically by author and has no indexes.

379.  Ingersoll, Jasper; Nancy Walstrom Jabbra; and Barbara Lenkerd. Resettlement and Settlement: An Annotated Bibliography. SEADAG Papers on Problems of Development in Southeast Asia, 76-1. New York: The Asia Society, [1976?] 30 leaves.
     Monographs, journal articles, government and UN documents as well as unpublished research papers and dissertations are included in this bibliography. The bibliography is organized into three sections: "Forced Resettlement from Reservoirs," "Other Resettlement," and "Settlement and Colonization." Within each section entries are arranged by author.
     The bibliography is not limited by geographical region or date of publication. There are no indexes.

380.  International Labour Organization. Bibliography of Rural Migration for Selected Developing Countries 1960-1970. Geneva: ILO, 1970. ii + 41p.
     This bibliography was prepared for the 1970 session of the Working Party on Rural Sociological Problems in Europe of the European Commission for Agriculture. It revises and updates a previous work entitled Bibliography of Rural Migration 1960-1968 for Selected Developing Countries. Several languages are represented in the works cited which date, with few exceptions, from 1960 to 1970.
     "The entries, starting with a general list, are arranged in alphabetical order and on a regional basis. Each

of the main lists (Africa, Asia, Oceania, Latin America and
the Caribbean) is preceded by a bibliography of regional and/
or subregional studies pertaining to two or more countries
in the region." There are no indexes.

381. Lex, Barbara W. From South to North: Cityward Mi-
     gration of Low Income Whites in the Twentieth Cen-
     tury. Pt. 1. Exchange Bibliography, nos. 907-
     908. Pt. 2. Exchange Bibliography, nos. 909-910.
     Monticello, IL: Council of Planning Librarians,
     1975. 169p.
     In this extensive bibliography the compiler states
that, "working within an anthropological perspective, I have
tended to select materials which are drawn from small-scale
research in rural countries, towns or neighborhoods....
One of my major objectives is to acquaint anthropologists
with the numerous studies of rural localities which have been
generated by rural sociologists who are affiliated with Agricultural Experiment Stations."
     Including books, articles, government documents
and technical reports, dissertations, and theses published in
this century, the bibliography is organized into 86 subject
divisions including community life, family life, migration, and
poverty among many others. Entries are arranged by author
within each subject division. There are no indexes.

382. Meyer, Paul A., and Colin MacAndrews. Transmigra-
     tion in Indonesia: An Annotated Bibliography. PI-
     GMU Bibliography Series, no. 3. Yogyakarta:
     Gadjah Mada University Press, 1978. 245p.
     Transmigration in Indonesia concerns government
efforts to move people from heavily populated to less populated areas. This bibliography includes all works (except
newspaper articles) on the subject available in Indonesian
libraries in 1976. Citations to English language publications
are a significant but minority portion of the bibliography.
     After introductory chapters on "Background Materi-
als," "Program Planning," and "Activity Reports," the bibliography is arranged by geographical region and then by author. Appendices include contents of the journal Transmig-
rasi, 1953-1958, "Index of Authors," "Glossary," and "Address of Libraries Visited."

383. Moore, Carolynne. Out-Migration in Appalachia: An
     Annotated Bibliography. Exchange Bibliography,

no. 1024. Monticello, IL: Council of Planning Librarians, 1976. 32p.
Articles, papers, books, dissertations, and government documents, dating primarily from the 1950's and later,
are listed in this bibliography. The bibliography begins with
entries on the subject of rural-urban migration in general and
then continues to sections on Appalachian life and migration
from it. The bibliography concludes with an unannotated
list of related sources. Within subject divisions entries are
arranged by author. There are no indexes.

384. Price, Daniel O., and Melanie M. Sikes. Rural-Urban
      Migration Research in the United States: Annotated
      Bibliography and Synthesis. Bethesda, MD: Cen-
      ter for Population Research, U.S. Dept. of Health,
      Education, and Welfare, 1975. 250p.
      This bibliography lists works on migration in the
U.S. from rural to urban areas published, with few exceptions, between 1950 and 1972. Monographs, government reports, periodical articles, etc., as well as dissertations and
other unpublished research papers, are included. Issues
covered include "sources and selectivity of migration and effects on rural areas; the decision to migrate; adjustment of
migrants and effects on urban areas; the characteristics of
return migrants; and needed research indicated by major
gaps in knowledge in this field.
      "The bulk of the volume, Part II, consists of an
'Annotated Bibliography' arranged alphabetically by author.
Part I represents the 'Synthesis of Research' based on findings in Part II, and Part III, the 'Topical Index,' provides
a key to listings by subject matter."

385. Suval, Elizabeth M. Selectivity in Migration: A Re-
      view of the Literature. Technical Bulletin, no. 209.
      Raleigh: North Carolina Experiment Station, 1972.
      79p.
      The literature review and concluding bibliography
are limited to research on migration in the United States and
emphasize migration within and from rural areas. Books,
journal articles, dissertations, and government documents
(especially Experiment Station publications) are all included.
Arrangement is by author and the bibliography is not limited
by date of publication.

## NOMADISM

386. Baumer, Michel, and Edmund Bernus. "A Selective
    Bibliography on Nomadism in the Sahelo-Saharian
    and Sahelo-Sudanian Zones," Arid Lands Newsletter 10 (April 1979):19-26.
    Nearly 350 works in either French or English are
listed without restriction by date of publication. The bibliography is organized into a general section on nomadism in
the Sahelo-Saharian and Sahelo-Sudanian region and then by
region: "Mauritania and Senegal," "Mali and Upper Volta,"
"Niger, Nigeria and Southern Algerian Sahara," and "Chad
and the Sudan."

387. Oxby, Clare. Pastoral Nomads and Development: A
    Select Annotated Bibliography with Special Reference
    to the Sahel, with an Analytical Introduction in English and French. London: International African
    Institute, 1975. 35p.
    Books, periodical articles, research papers and UN
documents are included in this bibliography of works in English or French. The bibliography is not limited by date of
publication, although most citations are to works published
after 1960.
    The bibliography is intended as a practical guide to
the literature and was compiled at the request of Christian
Aid. The author begins the bibliography with an introduction to nomadism and the issues surrounding development
programs intended to improve their lives. The bibliography
is organized into three parts. Part I is "Recent Collections
of Articles" in which ten collections published between 1959
and 1974 are analyzed in terms of number of articles, geographical coverage, availability in London libraries, and language of publication. Part II is "An Annotated Selection of
Articles" and includes some of the articles cited in Part I.
Part III is an unannotated list that includes some works cited

in Parts I and II. This section is the most extensive and is
divided into three subject sections: "Traditional Pastoral
Nomadic Societies and Unplanned Change," "Planned Change:
The Settlement of Pastoral Nomads," and "Planned Change:
The Modernisation of Pastoralism." There are no indexes.

388. Young, William. The Bedouin of Sinai, with a Bibli-
     ography on Settlement and Development in Pastoral
     Nomadic Areas of Africa and the Middle East Com-
     piled by George Ngugi. Fourth World Studies in
     Planning, no. 16. Los Angeles: School of Archi-
     tecture and Urban Planning, University of Califor-
     nia, [1981?].

     Books, parts of books, journal articles, research
papers, theses, and UN reports are listed by author in the
11-page bibliography that appears at the end of this work.

PEASANTRY

389. Benito, Carlos A. Peasant Economies and Rural De-
velopment--An Annotated Bibliography. Working
Paper, no. 78. Berkeley: California Agricultural
Experiment Station, Giannini Foundation of Agricul-
tural Economics, University of California, 1979.
23p.
This bibliography is composed of five reading lists
--"Introduction to Peasant Studies," "Economics of Peasants
--Household Level," "Economics of Peasants--Social Class
Level," "Rural Development Programs," and "Quantitative
Methods." Books and journal articles from the 1960's and
1970's are emphasized in each of the selected lists.

390. Farmers Assistance Board. Bibliography on the Peasantry. Quezon City, The Philippines: The Board,
1979. 27p.
The peasantry in the Philippines is emphasized in
this partially annotated bibliography but other countries are
represented as well. Arrangement is alphabetical by author
with no subject divisions or indexes.

391. Freebairn, Donald K.; Mariann Loveland; and Elyse
Tepper. An Annotated Bibliography of Writings on
Peasant Economy. Cornell Agricultural Economics
Staff Paper, no. 80-29. Ithaca, NY: Dept. of Ag-
ricultural Economics, Cornell University Agricultural
Experiment Station, 1980. 51p.
Items in this bibliography were selected from World
Agricultural Economics and Rural Sociology Abstracts, 1970-
1979. Arrangement is by author within seven chapters--
"Case Studies of the Peasantry," "Politics and the Peasan-
try," "The Theory of Peasant Economy," "Historical Process
in Peasant Economies," "Production Organization and the
Peasantry," "Agrarian Structure," and "Peasant Movements."
There are no indexes.

392.  Gutkind, Peter C.W., and Dimitrios Papadopoulos.
      "Third World Peasantries:  A Select Bibliography,"
      Peasant Studies 12, no. 1 (1984):31-89.
      Arrangement in this extensive bibliography of pub-
lished works is by author within sixteen subject divisions.
Subject headings include "Theoretical Perspectives on 'Peasantry,'" "Peasantry as a Cultural System," "Peasants and
Politics," "Agrarian and Land Reform," etc.  There is a
concluding geographical index.

393.  Kee Kum Ping, et al.  Bibliografi kaum Tani dan
      Pembangunan di Kawasan Asean / Bibliography on
      Peasantry and Development in the Asean Region.
      Bangi, Malaysia:  Perpustakaan Universiti Kebang-
      saan Malaysia, 1980.  xxiii + 222p.
      This is an extensive bibliography of both published
and unpublished materials, most of which were written in the
1970's.  The bibliography is the ninth in a series of General
Bibliographies published by the Universiti Kebangsaan Malaysia Library.
      "The bibliography is organized into broad subject
divisions starting with a review of the literature on development strategies and policies in the Asean region in general
and in each country in particular.  This is followed by literature on development and the economics of production (land,
labour, capital, farm organization, new technology, types of
farming and marketing), collectives and cooperatives, extension services, and finally, literature on the sociological implications of development on the peasantry.  All citations are
arranged alphabetically by author and/or title."  There are
no indexes.

394.  Marshall, Trevor G.  A Bibliography of the Common-
      wealth Caribbean Peasantry, 1838-1974.  Occasional
      Bibliography Series, no. 3.  Cave Hill, Barbados:
      Institute of Social and Economic Research (Eastern
      Caribbean), University of the West Indies, 1975.
      vi + 47 leaves.
      Books, journal articles, conference proceedings,
theses, dissertations, unpublished papers, and government
documents are all included in this bibliography on rural
Caribbean life.  Part I concerns the Caribbean in general,
Part II individual territories.  In Part I and under larger
territories in Part II, entries are arranged under sub-
headings of "Economic," "Sociological," and "Historical."

Within these divisions arrangement is alphabetical by author.
There are no indexes.

395. Sanders, Irwin; Roger Whitaker; and Walter C. Bis-
     selle. East European Peasantries:  Social Relations;
     An Annotated Bibliography of Periodical Articles.
     Boston:  G.K. Hall. Vol. 1, 1976.  vi + 179p.;
     Vol. 2, 1981, ix + 200p.
     "The titles included in this bibliography refer to
periodical articles collected and bound in thirty volumes by
countries.  They are available in the Reference Room of the
Mugar Library at Boston University."  The bibliography includes works in several languages; the annotations are in
English.  Although the bibliography is not limited by date,
most entries were published after 1960.  The bibliography is
organized by country and then by author.  There are no
indexes.  Volume II lists more than 850 additions to the collection since the publication of the first volume.

396. Schendel, Willem Van. Bangladesh:  A Bibliography
     with Special Reference to the Peasantry.  Voor-
     publikatie, no. 10.  Amsterdam:  Afdeling Zuid- en
     Zuidoost-Azië Antropologisch-Sociologisch Centrum,
     University of Amsterdam, 1976.  ix + 227p.
     The compiler has emphasized "socio-cultural, his-
torical and socio-economic conditions of the population of
rural Bangladesh...."  Books, journal articles, dissertations
as well as other published and unpublished sources are included without limitation by date.  Most works are in English although other European languages are represented.
     The bibliography is organized into several subject
chapters within which arrangement is alphabetical by author.
The main section was compiled in 1974; there is a concluding
supplement compiled in 1975.  The compiler also provides a
list of source journals and an index by name.

397. Scott, James C., and Howard Leichter. A Bibliography
     on Land, Peasants, and Politics for Burma and
     Thailand.  Land Tenure Center Special Bibliography.
     [Madison:  Land Tenure Center, University of Wis-
     consin], 1972.
     The compilers state that they "have tried to empha-
size those studies which deal with social structure and peasant politics.  The bibliography will therefore be of most value
to those scholars who wish to relate economic change to social

structure and politics. Purely technical studies and crop
research have not been included."
      Arrangement is by author under topic headings
within each of the two countries covered. There are 466
citations to works on Thailand and 88 to works on Burma.
A wide range of material, not restricted by date of publication, is included.

398.  Scott, James C., and Howard Leichter. A Bibliography
      on Land, Peasants, and Politics for Malaysia, In-
      donesia, and the Philippines. Land Tenure Center
      Special Bibliography. Madison: Land Tenure Cen-
      ter, University of Wisconsin, 1972.
      The 475 items in this bibliography include a wide
range of material--journal articles, dissertations, government
publications, etc.--and are not restricted by date of publication. Each of the three countries is a separate section of
the bibliography and within each section arrangement is by
author under 14 subject divisions. The divisions include
"Agrarian Economy," "Peasant Economics," "Land Reform,"
"Land Tenure," etc. There are no indexes.

399.  Scott, James C., and Howard Leichter. A Bibliography
      on Land, Peasants, and Politics for Viet-Nam, Laos,
      and Cambodia. Land Tenure Center Special Bibliog-
      raphy. [Madison: Land Tenure Center, University
      of Wisconsin], 1972.
      This bibliography is comparable in scope to the
compilers' other bibliographies on land, peasants, and politics in Asian countries. Most of the bibliography is devoted to Vietnam with smaller sections on Cambodia and Laos.
Under each country arrangement is by author within topic
headings--"Land Reform," "Peasant Economies," etc. There
is no restriction by date of publication.

400.  Watson, Charlotte B. Bibliography on Peasant Move-
      ments. Prepared for the Savannah Conference,
      June 3-6, 1974. 36 leaves.
      This unpublished bibliography is available at the
Land Tenure Center Library, University of Wisconsin-
Madison. Partially annotated, it lists both published and
unpublished works in one alphabetical list by author. There
is no restriction by date or geographical region.

# TRANSPORTATION

401. Banister, David. Rural Transport and Planning: A
     Bibliography with Abstracts. London: Mansell,
     1985. vi + 448p.
     This is a comprehensive bibliography organized
into seven major sections: "The Context," "Policy and
planning in transport," "Accessibility and mobility," "Transport modes," "Methods and evaluation," "Area-based studies," and "Bibliographies." "Each section has a short introduction that attempts to describe and highlight the main
themes together with the principal publications." Annotations are extensive. There are concluding subject and author indexes.

402. Bebee, Charles N. Transporting Commodities and Ru-
     ral People. Quick Bibliography Series, no. 79-32.
     Beltsville, MD: National Agricultural Library, 1979.
     The 279 citations in this bibliography are English
language publications from the Agricola data base for the
years 1969 to 1978. While most of the references concern
transporting agricultural products, a significant minority,
mostly Experiment Station publications, deals with transportation as a social issue for rural populations.

403. California Dept. of Transportation. Rural Intercity
     Bus Systems: A Bibliography. Sacramento: Bus
     and Paratransit Branch, Division of Mass Trans-
     portation, California Dept. of Transportation, 1978.
     6 leaves.
     State and federal documents and reports, unpub-
lished papers, and research reports constitute the majority
of entries in this bibliography, although some books, periodical articles, and newspaper articles are also included.
Most items were published in the 1970's.

404.  Great Britain.  Dept. of the Environment and Dept. of
        Transport.  Roads and Transport in Rural Areas.
        Compiled by Joan Alletson.  Bibliography, no. 17b.
        London:  Dept. of the Environment, 1976.  23p.
    All aspects of the rural transportation problem in
the United Kingdom are discussed.  Major sections of the
bibliography are "Books and Pamphlets," "Articles," and
"Research in Progress."  Within sub-sections material is arranged chronologically.  Most citations are to works published in the 1970's.  A 1983 supplement titled Rural Transport, 1977-1983 updates this work.

405.  Krummes, Daniel C.  Rural Transit:  An Annotated
        Bibliography.  Berkeley, CA:  Institute of Trans-
        portation Studies, University of California, 1983.
        31p.
    "This annotated bibliography concerns multimodal
rural transit in the United States and Canada, with some
reference to Western Europe.  The emphasis is on intercity
bus lines and paratransit services, though a few works on
railroad passenger service are included.  Also included are
periodicals, general works, other bibliographies, and information on the planning and management of rural transit services.  Nearly 75 case studies of existing rural transit systems are presented as well as a geographical index to cited
works."
    Arrangement is by author within subjects such as
"Planning," "Management," "Case Studies," etc.  Most works
cited were published in the late 1970's or early 1980's.

406.  Moseley, Malcolm; Oliver Coles; and Gwen Hughes.
        "An Annotated Bibliography" in Rural Transport
        and Accessibility.  Vol. 2.  Appendices and Anno-
        tated Bibliography.  Norwich, U.K.:  Centre of
        East Anglian Studies, University of East Anglia,
        1977, pp. 90-184.
    This bibliography was prepared in conjunction with
a research project contracted by the U.K. Dept. of the Environment, the final report of which was published as Volume I of Rural Transport and Accessibility.  Most of the
entries in the bibliography were published in the 1970's and
relate to Great Britain.  While some concern Europe or North
America, none concerns rural transport in the Third World.
    "Many of the references might be termed 'semi-
published material.'  There are academic theses, local

government memoranda, discussion papers of various sorts--
as well as conventionally published books, journal articles
and official reports."

Organized into several subject divisions such as
"Rural Society," "The Rural Elderly and Disadvantaged,"
"Rural Accessibility Studies," etc., the bibliography ends
with both author and place indexes.

407. Rural Passenger Transportation Primer:  Selected
     Transportation Topics.  [Washington, D.C.]:  Of-
     fice of R & D Policy, U.S. Dept. of Transportation,
     1977.  iii + 70p.

The emphasis in this annotated bibliography is on
state and federal government documents and technical reports.
Some periodical articles, conference proceedings, etc. are
also included.  Most publications date from the 1970's although
a few are from the late 1960's.

The first section of this work is devoted to an
overview of transportation in rural America.  The bibliography
itself is organized into sections on "Needs," "Planning/Manage-
ment," "Programs," and "General Information."  It concludes
with an author index and an organization index.

408. Cebotarev, E.A., et al. "An Annotated Bibliography on Women in Agriculture and Rural Societies," Resources for Feminist Research 11, no. 1 (March 1982):93-180.

Included in an issue of Resources for Feminist Research devoted entirely to women in agriculture and rural society, this bibliography lists a wide range of "published and unpublished documents from both academic and nonacademic sources. The works cited are grouped into four major sections: Canada, Other Industrialized Countries, Developing Countries, and General Worldwide. These four sections are broken down into regions and countries where appropriate."

Works in the first two sections emphasize women's involvement with family farms. Works on rural women in developing countries are much broader in scope and include studies of rural women's nutrition, family planning, etc. The concluding section not only lists theoretical and empirical works relevant to rural women in developed and developing countries but also bibliographies, manuals, organizations, and periodicals.

"The work cited in the Canadian section was not limited to a time period; however, the work cited in the other three sections, with very few exceptions was published after 1975."

409. Commonwealth Bureau of Agricultural Economics. Women in Rural Development. Annotated Bibliography, no. RDA2/Q51. Commonwealth Agricultural Bureaux.

Unavailable for annotation. Secondary sources indicate that the bibliography covers CAB indexes for 1978-82 and lists 400 citations.

410. Craig, R.A. Rural Women--An Annotated Bibliography

of Australian Sources. Roseworthy, South Australia:
Dept. of Extension and Education, Roseworthy Agri-
cultural College, 1980.
Unavailable for annotation.

411. Fassinger, Polly. Women in Agriculture: A Bibliogra-
phy. East Lansing: Sociology Dept., Michigan
State University, forthcoming.
Unavailable for annotation.

412. Food and Agriculture Organization of the United Nations. Documentation Centre and Population Documentation Centre. Women and Family in Rural Development: Annotated Bibliography. Rome: FAO,
1977. viii + 41p. + 2p. + 15p.
This bibliography lists FAO publications issued from
1966 to mid-1976. Several languages are represented. Arranged by accession number, it is difficult to use except
through the analytical index. The annotations are brief
synopses with embedded descriptors. There is an author
index as well as the analytical index.

413. Fortmann, Louise. Tillers of the Soil and Keepers of
the Hearth: A Bibliographic Guide to Women and
Rural Development. Ithaca, NY: Rural Development
Committee, Center for International Studies, Cornell
University, 1979.
The focus of this bibliography is post-1970 literature emphasizing "the practical and the case study rather
than more theoretical works." The bibliography emphasizes
but is not limited to the Third World. A wide range of
published and unpublished literature is included.
The bibliography is organized first into a section of
bibliographies followed by one on readers. The latter gives
tables of contents and is intended to aid teachers in judging
the appropriateness of titles for courses. The subject chapters that follow are titled "General," "Agriculture," "Economic Participation," "Education," "Law," "Family," "Population," and "Ethnography." Within chapters arrangement is
alphabetical by author. There is an index by country or
region.

414. Fowler, Becky. Rural Women: An Annotated Bibliog-
raphy, 1976-1979. Morgantown: Rural Community
Development Learning Center, School of Social Work,
West Virginia University, 1979. 26p. ED 187 498.

This "annotated bibliography provides general information regarding rural women in the United States from 1976 to 1979. It contains citations for 113 articles, books, bibliographies, papers and monographs. Citations are organized alphabetically by author or title in seven categories: agriculture; Appalachia and the South; education; health and mental health; industry and the labor force; music, literature and the arts; and national perspectives and policies regarding rural women."

415. Henderson, Francine I. Women in Botswana: An Annotated Bibliography. Working Bibliography, no. 4. Gaborone: Documentation Unit, National Institute of Development and Cultural Research, University College of Botswana, 1981. 20p.
    Published and unpublished research material on women in Botswana is arranged in one list by author. Citations do not always provide complete bibliographical information. Each citation indicates in which library in Botswana the item can be located. Most, though not all, items specifically concern rural women. The bibliography ends with a selected list of works relating to rural women in places other than Botswana. There are no indexes.

416. Inter-American Institute of Agricultural Sciences. Committee for Rural Women and Development. Rural Women: A Caribbean Bibliography with Special Reference to Jamaica. Documentación e Información Agricola, no. 82. San José, Costa Rica: The Institute, 1980. 29 leaves.
    This bibliography is organized into three sections. The first lists a selection of background readings on women and development, the second is on rural women in Jamaica, and the third is on Jamaican women in general. Each of the last two sections has further subject sub-divisions. The bibliography is partially annotated and contains citations to both published and unpublished works without restriction by date. There is a concluding author index.

417. Joyce, Lynda. Annotated Bibliography of Women in Rural America with a Review of the Literature about Women in Rural America, Bibliography of Women in Rural Areas Worldwide, and Resource Material. A.E. & R.S., no. 125. University Park, PA: Dept. of Agricultural Economics and Rural Sociology,

Agricultural Experiment Station, The Pennsylvania
State University, 1976. 62 leaves.
This bibliography varies only slightly from the one
included in the author's 1977 publication.

418.  Joyce, Lynda M., and Samuel M. Leadley.  An Assess-
      ment of Research Needs of Women in the Rural
      United States: Literature Review and Annotated
      Bibliography. A.E. & R.S., no. 127. University
      Park, PA: Dept. of Agricultural Economics and
      Rural Sociology, The Pennsylvania State Univer-
      sity, 1977. 116 leaves. ED 141 465.
Approximately half of this work is devoted to a review of the research literature on women in rural America.
The second half is devoted to bibliographic appendices. The
first, "The Annotated Bibliography of Women in Rural America," includes all items referred to in the review of research.
Other appendices are: "Supplementary List to the Annotated
Bibliography by date of Publication," "Bibliography of Women
in Rural Areas Worldwide, 1967-1975," "Bibliographic Addendum (which includes items related to but not specifically on
the subject of rural women as well as items that the compilers could not locate for review)," "Bibliography of Bibliographies of Women in Rural America," and "Periodicals Concerning Women in Rural America."
      All sections but one are arranged by author. The
Supplementary Bibliographic list is arranged by date from
1975-76 to 1900, the cut-off date for inclusion in the bibliography. The bibliographies include books, articles, proceedings, ERIC documents, and government documents.
There are no indexes.

419.  Kestner, Jean.  Women in Rural Society. Common-
      wealth Bureau of Agricultural Economics, Annotated
      Bibliography, no. 15. Commonwealth Agricultural
      Bureaux. Rev. ed., 1975. 9p.
      The 73 items in this revised bibliography were pub-
lished between 1968 and 1974 and appear to have been selected from CAB indexing journals. After an initial section
on "International Aspects," the bibliography is arranged by
country and author. Both developed and developing countries are included.

420.  Lear, Julia Graham.  Rural Development: Recognizing
      the Role of Women; A Select Bibliography.

Prepared for the Committee on Women in Development, Society for International Development. Washington, D.C., 1974. 7 leaves. Draft. This brief bibliography, available at the University of Wisconsin-Madison, Land Tenure Center Library, is arranged by author under sections on books, periodicals, manuscripts and monographs, and official documents (which lists UN publications). Most of the citations are to works published in the early 1970's.

421.    McCarthy, Florence E.; Saleh Sabbah; and Roushan Akhter. Bibliography and Selected References Regarding Rural Women in Bangladesh. Dacca: Women's Section, Planning and Development Division, Ministry of Agriculture, 1978. 44 leaves. ED 218 035.
       Organized into several subject chapters such as development, law, and village life, this bibliography includes a variety of types of material but emphasizes unpublished and published research reports from the 1970's. Some subject areas, e.g., working women, include information not restricted to rural areas. Likewise, in other subject areas information is included on social and economic conditions affecting rural men as well as women. The bibliography concludes with an author index.

422.    Moser, Collette, and Deborah Johnson. Rural Women Workers in the 20th Century: An Annotated Bibliography. Special Paper, no. 15. East Lansing: Center for Rural Manpower and Public Affairs, Michigan State University, 1973. 63p. NTIS, PB-226487. ED 100 570.
       Items listed in this bibliography were readily available at the Michigan State University Library and the Michigan State Library. Most of the items listed concern rural U.S. women.
       "The first section of the bibliography is concerned with preparations for work and includes two categories: 'Investment in Human Resources; Education, Counselling, Training, and Labor Market Information' and 'Investment in Human Resources: Migration and Mobility.' "
       The next section is devoted to farm work and is divided into two categories: "Labor Force Participation--Quantitative" and "Labor Force Participation--Qualitative."
       Section three is devoted to problems of working for

rural women. The fourth section deals with relevant organizations and the concluding sections with "Fertility, Population, Demography and Trends," "Rural Development and Economic Change," and "Rural Life, Miscellaneous." The bibliography concludes with a sampling of information available
on international trends concerning rural women. There are
no indexes.

423. Nelson, Nici. Why Has Development Neglected Rural
     Women? A Review of the South Asian Literature.
     Women in Development, vol. 1. Oxford, U.K.:
     Pergamon Press, 1979. 108p.

     The author reviews what she believes to be the
inadequate research literature on rural women in Bangladesh,
Pakistan, India, and Sri Lanka. Not claiming to have a
neutral stance, she states that "the purpose of this review
is to convince those researchers interested in rural women
or in rural development to widen the scope of their concern
to investigate the roles women currently have, and should
have in the future, in the process of rural development tak-
ing place in South Asia...."
     The review discusses the extant research literature
and what has been learned from it and then recommends
areas for future research. The concluding bibliography contains both published and unpublished works. "The sources
in the bibliography all include data on, or theoretical analysis of, women, particularly rural women; most of them refer
directly to development issues. Sources dealing with areas
other than South Asia are included only where relevant."
Most but not all items in the bibliography are discussed in
the review.

424. Rafats, Jerry. Women's Role in Farming and Agricul-
     ture. Quick Bibliography Series, no. 84-64. Belts-
     ville, MD: National Agricultural Library, 1984.
     10p.

     The 113 citations in this partially annotated bibli-
ography were compiled from the Agricola data base and update a 1982 publication of the same title. There is no restriction by geographical region. There is a concluding
author index.

425. Skamay-Meeks, Adriana. Women's Role in Farming and
     Agriculture, 1970-August 1982. Quick Bibliography
     Series, no. 83-05. Beltsville, MD: National Agri-
     cultural Library, 1982. 9p.

The 166 citations in this partially annotated bibliography result from a computer search of the Agricola data
base. The format is a reproduction of the computer print-
out. There is no geographical limitation. There is a concluding author index. An update with the same title was
compiled in 1984.

426.  Suvanajata, Titaya, et al.  Selected Bibliography from
      the U.N. Agencies Libraries in Bangkok on Rural
      Women in Asia.  Bangkok:  Research Center, The
      National Institute of Development Administration,
      1979.  ii + 84p.
          Books, UN documents, and journal articles are
      listed along with many papers presented at conferences,
      workshops and seminars.  Most date from the 1970's.
          Entries are annotated and after a general section
      are arranged by country and then author.  There are no
      indexes.

427.  Suvanajata, Titaya, et al.  Selected Bibliography with
      Annotations from the U.N. Libraries in Bangkok on
      Rural Women in Asia.  Bangkok:  National Institute
      of Development Administration, [1981?]  144p.
      Unavailable for annotation.

428.  University of Wisconsin.  Land Tenure Center Library.
      Women in Rural Development:  A Bibliography.
      Training & Methods Series, no. 29.  Madison:  Land
      Tenure Center Library, 1979.  45p.
          This bibliography lists material on women and rural
      development available in the Land Tenure Center Library.
      With few exceptions, the works included were published in
      the 1970's.  The bibliography includes a wide range of ma-
      terial and is arranged, after an introductory general sec-
      tion, by continent, country, and author.  There are no in-
      dexes.  A call number or other information to provide loca-
      tion within the Land Tenure Center Library has been pro-
      vided for each item.

429.  Wheat, Valerie, and Judi Conrad.  Rural Women and
      Education:  Annotated Selected References and Re-
      sources.  Bibliography Series, no. 6.  Las Cruces:
      Educational Resources Information Center, Clearing-
      house on Rural Education and Small Schools, New
      Mexico State University, 1978.  30p.  ED 160 334.

"Both literature and organizational citations are included in this annotated bibliography on rural women.  Literature citations range between 1939 and 1977, with the majority of the citations representing literature published in
the 70's."  Arrangement is by title within subject divisions
such as "Rural Women:  Historical and Contemporary Perspectives," "Rural Women:  Educational, Occupational and
Personal Aspirations," "Rural Women:  Education," "Rural
Women at Work," etc.

430. Aspirations of Rural Youth: A Selected Topics Bibliography of ERIC Documents. Las Cruces: Educational Resources Information Center, Clearinghouse on Rural Education and Small Schools, New Mexico State University, 1977. 17p. ED 153 760.
"... This bibliography contains resource material and research findings about aspirational needs of rural youth--including ethnic, male/female and urban/rural comparisons. The 10 citations, published from 1966 to 1974, are drawn from Resources in Education...."

431. Educational and Occupational Aspirations of Rural Youth: A Selected Topics Bibliography of ERIC Documents. Las Cruces: Educational Resources Information Center, Clearinghouse on Rural Education and Small Schools, New Mexico State University, 1977. 89p. ED 153 772.
"... This annotated bibliography includes 116 citations on the educational and occupational aspirations and expectations of rural youth. Citations are derived from ... 'Resources in Education' (RIE) and 'Current Index to Journals in Education' (CIJE). The RIE citations cover the period June 1967 through March 1977. The CIJE citations cover the period January 1970 through March 1977.... Major concepts covered include: racial differences; rural urban differences; employment opportunities; educational status comparisons; achievement needs; socioeconomic status; dropouts; career choice; social mobility; changing attitudes; and values."

432. Rural Youth Expectations: A Selected Topics Bibliography of ERIC Documents. Las Cruces: Educational Resources Information Center, Clearinghouse on Rural Education and Small Schools, New Mexico State University, 1977. 42p. ED 153 764.

"... The 42 (annotated) citations on rural youth
cover expectations and aspirations about education, occupa-
tion, residence, marriage, and procreation ... and focus on
such influences as race, sex, socio-economic status, and
residence. All are based on U.S. data. The citations, published between 1968 and 1976, come from 'Resources in Education' ... and from 'Current Index to Journals in Education.' "

433. Socioeconomic and Social Aspects of Rural Youth:  A
      Selected Topics Bibliography of ERIC Documents.
      Las Cruces:  Educational Resources Information
      Center, Clearinghouse on Rural Education and
      Small Schools, New Mexico State University, 1977.
      66p.  ED 153 762.
      "... The socioeconomic and social aspects of rural
youth both in the U.S. and internationally are cited in this
bibliography of ERIC documents...." Annotated items from
Resources in Education and Current Index to Journals in
Education are included.  Publication dates range from 1960
to 1976.

434. Ziche, Joachim.  "Rural Youth:  A Review of Research
      Literature," World Agricultural Economics and Rural
      Sociology Abstracts 18, no. 7 (July 1976):415-428.
      A wide range of works published between the early
1950's and mid-1970's is included in this bibliography.  English is only one of several languages represented.  In the
review of the literature the author first discusses "Studies
of an all-inclusive type at the national or international level"
and "Studies of an all-inclusive type at the local or regional
level."  This is followed by discussion of works on specific
issues surrounding rural youth--e.g., motivations, aspirations, employment, etc.  The bibliography lists 279 items
alphabetically by author.

# PERSONAL AND CORPORATE NAME INDEX

# TITLE INDEX

# GEOGRAPHICAL INDEX